THE LAWS OF POWER

BRIAN TRACY

THE LAWS OF POWER

HOW TO USE TIME-TESTED TRUTHS TO GET EVERYTHING YOU WANT

MEDIA

Published 2024 by Gildan Media LLC
aka G&D Media
www.GandDmedia.com

Front cover design by David Rheinhardt of Pyrographx

Interior design by Meghan Day Healey of Story Horse, LLC

Library of Congress Cataloging-in-Publication Data is available upon request

ISBN: 978-1-7225-0696-4

10 9 8 7 6 5 4 3 2 1

Contents

Foreword   vii

one The Laws of Success   1

two The Laws of Achievement   27

three The Laws of Happiness   55

four The Laws of Relationships   75

five The Laws of Economics   97

six The Laws of Negotiating   121

seven The Laws of Money   143

eight The Laws of Wealth Creation   165

nine The Laws of Sales   185

ten The Laws of Business   207

eleven The Laws of Luck   235

twelve The Laws of Self-Fulfillment   255

Contents

Foreword

Throughout the ages, human beings have attempted to make sense of the universe, unravel mysteries that have challenged their intellects, and seek solutions to seemingly unsolvable puzzles.

In looking for the truth and often questioning it, poets, thinkers, philosophers, and scientists have immeasurably influenced our world. Their medical breakthroughs, scientific discoveries, physical laws, and mathematical principles have imposed order, coherence and clarity to what once seemed a random, indiscriminate, and lawless world.

The driving force behind these great thinkers often was their innate desire to succeed, to focus their minds on a question and strive relentlessly until they found the answer. In their wealth of wisdom, we now find universal principles of personal success and achievement that we can use to maximize our own potential.

These success principles are as timeless and immutable as the physical laws governing the universe. They hold true for everyone who abides by them and are applicable in almost every area of life. Never before have they all been brought together as a vital tool for teaching. Never before has all this information been combined to give you a guaranteed formula for success, until now.

Brian Tracy has devoted almost his entire life to studying success and human development, and he is a living example of the practical principles he teaches. In this book, you'll learn about the success principles that have been the hallmark of all great achievers. Brian calls them "universal laws" because they work for anyone, anywhere, anytime, and they will work for you. All you need to do is apply, practice, and follow them consciously as you set and move toward your goals, and the results you desire will come to you: business success, wealth, happiness, self-fulfillment, love, and relationships. These are just some of the areas that you'll be able to improve in your life as you learn and apply these universal laws of success and achievement.

one

The Laws of Success

Throughout history, most of the smartest men believed that it was not possible for any object heavier than air to fly. Then a professor at the University of Basel, Daniel Bernoulli, laid down a series of hydrodynamic principles, including his most famous: a complex principle of air resistance, which has come to be known as Bernoulli's law. The application of Bernoulli's law to aeronautical engineering led to the first flight by the Wright brothers at Kitty Hawk in 1903 and to the entire world of modern aviation as we now know it today.

Daniel Bernoulli didn't invent this law, but once he discovered it and others learned to apply it, humans were able to conquer the skies. Today planes can fly almost anywhere in the world at several hundred miles an hour with a speed and efficiency that was unimaginable even a hundred years ago—all because of Bernoulli's law.

You too can fly. By using the laws and principles of success and achievement that have been discovered over the last 4,000 years, you can reach the heights of your potential. You can travel faster and further toward the achievement of your dreams and aspirations than you ever dreamed possible. When you apply these proven and practical principles to your life, you'll begin to make progress you may have never imagined.

When you organize your life so that everything that you're thinking and doing is in harmony with the universal laws that predict and control human destiny, there'll be no limitations on what you can be and have and do.

When I was nineteen, I set out on a lifelong journey seeking the answers to the question, why are some people more successful than others? I came from a home where we never had very much money. I didn't finish high school, and I worked at laboring jobs for several years. I washed dishes, dug wells, and carried building materials on construction sites. I worked in factories and sawmills. I worked as a merchant seaman on a Norwegian freighter, and even as a farmhand during the harvest season.

Over the years, I traveled all over the world, studying different cultures, philosophies, religions, and schools of thought. Always I sought for the answers to that great question: why are some people more successful than others?

As the years passed and my experience accumulated, I noticed that there was a certain regularity and predictability in human events. There seemed to be laws and principles at work in almost everything that happened. I've now studied the subject for decades, and I've concluded that there are universal laws that anyone can use to dramatically enhance the quality of his or her life. They're available to you here in this book. When you apply them, you'll begin to get the things you want in every area of your life.

To state it simply, I discovered that successful people live their lives more in harmony with natural laws than unsuccessful people.

Successful and happy people consciously or unconsciously organize their thoughts, feelings, and actions in such a way that the powers available to them as a result of these laws seem to work for them. They go on to accomplish more in a few years than many people accomplish in a lifetime, simply because they do more things right and fewer things wrong. They make the right choices and decisions and take the right actions. They channel their mental, emotional, and physical energies toward attaining the things that enrich their lives. They waste very little of their time going down blind alleys or pursuing goals that ultimately lead to failure and frustration and lost months or years.

Successful people live their lives more in harmony with natural laws than unsuccessful people.

Successful people seem to live their lives more efficiently in moving from where they are to where they want to go. They seem to get there faster and easier and achieve greater satisfaction along the way.

Unsuccessful people, on the other hand, either don't know the universal laws or choose to ignore them in the short term, hoping that they'll be spared the consequences of their behavior in the long term. This attitude can lead to wasted years and unfulfilled lives. Whenever you see a person who's not achieving his or her full potential, you see a violation of universal laws that's both sad and unnecessary.

Universal laws are like physical laws such as the law of gravity. They're called laws because they're everywhere and always enforced, and ignorance of the law is no excuse. The law of gravity will work on you whether you step off a ten-story building in downtown New

York or in downtown London. You'll follow the law of gravity, gaining speed at 32 feet per second, as the law says, and you'll go splat on the sidewalk. It doesn't matter whether you know about gravity, whether you believe in gravity, whether anyone told you about how gravity works, or even whether or not gravity is particularly convenient for you at that moment. It will work on you in any case and you'll have to suffer the consequences.

Universal laws are not like man-made laws. A man-made law, like a traffic law, may or may not be enforced, depending upon the circumstances. You can break a traffic law and get away with it, at least in the short term. Universal laws are different. They work 100 percent of the time. Your job is to coordinate your thoughts and actions with them so that you're living your life in such a way that these laws are working on your behalf.

In this book, I'll introduce you to a series of laws that have been derived from experience, observation, and reflection. I'd like to say that I personally invented or discovered these laws, but that's not the case. They've been discovered and rediscovered throughout all the centuries of recorded time. These laws are applicable in a variety of ways and to a variety of situations. For instance, the same law, like the law of attraction, may apply in a slightly different form to achieving success, to happy relationships, and to wealth creation. The laws overlap and intertwine with each other. Sometimes one will take precedence over another, although none of them will ever really contradict the others.

Each chapter in this book explains a series of laws that apply especially to the chapter title, such as money and business, selling, and negotiating. Sometimes the laws will appear with more than one definition and you can apply them in several areas, for example, the laws of belief and correspondence.

The Law of Cause and Effect

The first law of success is the granddaddy of all laws, and it's the iron law of human destiny. We simply call it the *law of cause and effect*. This law governs the universe, and all other laws fall under it and are consistent with it. The law of cause and effect is referred to in the Bible as the law of sowing and reaping. The scientist Sir Isaac Newton referred to it as the law of action and reaction. Ralph Waldo Emerson called it the law of "compensation" in his famous essay of the same name. This law says that we live in an orderly universe, in which everything happens for a reason. There are no accidents, at least not in the long term. This law says that for every effect, there is a cause or a series of causes.

For every effect, there is a cause or a series of causes.

If there's an effect in your life that you desire, such as success or wealth or health or happiness, you can have it by simply instituting the causes that have been proven to generate it. This law also says that if there's an effect in your life that you don't particularly want, such as unhappiness, poor health, financial problems, or difficulties with other people, you can trace those effects back to their causes; by removing the causes, you can eliminate the effect.

This law is so simple that it's largely ignored and so common that the great majority of people attempt to live their lives in outright defiance of it. Even though they may not be happy with the results they're getting, they continue to repeat the same behaviors, which cause the same effects, and they become angry and frustrated when nothing changes. In fact, one definition of insanity is continuing to do the same things but expecting to get different results. You are surrounded by people who are getting effects that they don't want while not getting the effects they do want. They either don't realize or don't care that the only way to change the effects is to change the causes.

The law of cause and effect is a wonderful principle for lifelong success. It says that if you can clearly define the effect you desire; all you need to do is to find out who else has achieved the same effect and copy that person or persons until you get the same result. It's no mystery: if someone else has done it, you can probably do it as well, if you do the same things in the same way. The world is quite neutral about all this. The world, the marketplace, and other people don't really care who or what you are or where you come from as long as you institute the proven causes of the specific effects that you want. It doesn't matter if you're young or old, tall or short, black or white, male or female, fat or thin: nature plays no favorites. As the saying goes, the jungle is neutral; the playing field is level. If you repeatedly do the same things in the same way that other successful people have done, you'll eventually get the same results. Of course, a lot will depend upon how far back you're starting, but that's something you can always overcome by time and patience and determination.

A friend of mine who spent more than fifty years studying success concluded that one of the most important discoveries that he ever made was the necessity of using proven success principles. He said that if you're really serious about success, learn from the experts; spare no effort or expense to learn from those who have gone before you. He also said that life is too short for us to learn it all by ourselves. If you can find someone or several others who have achieved the result you desire, you learn from them what they did, and you do the same things repeatedly, you'll eventually get the same results yourself. If you sow the same seeds, you'll get the same harvest. If you duplicate the causes of the effects you desire and continue to do so in face of the inevitable discouragement that comes to all of us, you'll eventually get what you set out for. This is the law, and if you live your life in harmony with it, you can eventually attain things that will amaze everyone, including yourself.

The starting point of the application of the law of cause and effect is to clearly determine the effects that you desire.

Before you can apply the laws of success, you need to think seriously about what success means to you in the light of your unique past experiences, personality, abilities, values, beliefs, hopes, and aspirations. Only you can define what success means in your life. Success is sometimes defined as getting what you want. Others define success as the freedom to live your life in your own way without the interference of anyone else. You may define success as freedom from worries about material things. Someone else may define success in terms of happy and loving relationships. Another may define it in terms of health and mental and physical well-being. In any case, your first responsibility to yourself is to sit down and list all the things that would exist in your life if you finally achieved success.

With anything that you want to accomplish, you begin by defining your ideal result or your future vision for yourself. Even the shortest journey begins with deciding where you want to end up.

Before you begin selecting the causes you intend to initiate, you need to be extremely clear about the effects that you wish to realize. A woman who had been through my seminar on goal setting came to me afterwards and said that she had decided that her major goal was to sell a million dollars' worth of real estate. I asked her why she wanted that particular goal. She told me it was so that she could make enough money to get out of real estate completely and get into something that she really wanted to do. She was unhappy and frustrated and was not making much progress toward her goal. I explained to her that she'd never be happy or successful doing something that she didn't enjoy; perhaps she should change her direction and immediately begin doing something that she really cared about. Fortunately she accepted my advice and changed careers. The last time I saw her, she was happier than she had been in years.

This illustrates one of the most important applications of this law: in order to achieve certain effects, you must first instigate certain causes. Furthermore, in order to eliminate certain effects in your life, you must also eliminate the factors that are causing them.

The most important single application of the law of cause and effect is this: thoughts are causes, and conditions are effects. Your thoughts about any subject are the starting point of everything that happens to you. Your life conditions express your innermost thoughts and convictions. If you think a certain thought long enough and hard enough, it becomes a fixed belief, and you'll find yourself behaving on the outside in a manner consistent with it.

For example, if you think about success all the time and you think about the things that you can do to be more successful in the important areas of your life, your thoughts will lead you to the activities that will make that success much more possible for you. Your thoughts are the primary causes of the conditions of your life.

The Law of Mind

This brings us to the second of the laws of success: *the law of mind*. In its simplest form, it says that thoughts objectify themselves; thoughts held in mind produce after their kind. What you think becomes your reality. As Ralph Waldo Emerson observed, a man becomes what he thinks about most of the time. The law of mind is extremely powerful. It helps explain many of the other laws that refer to mind action.

The Law of Mental Equivalency

The natural extension of the law of mind is the third law of success: *the law of mental equivalency*. This law says that your primary responsibility to yourself is to create a clear and accurate mental equivalent of what you wish to experience in each dimension of your external life. If you want to be happy, you need to clearly define and create the mental equivalent or picture of exactly what happiness means to you. Similarly, if you wish to enjoy health, long life, happy relationships, or financial prosperity, you need to create in your mind an exact, detailed picture of what you desire. This becomes the critical starting point to realizing your dreams and goals.

The Law of Correspondence

The fourth law of success is called the *law of correspondence*. This law has been talked about for perhaps 4,000 years, and it's one of the fundamental laws that explain human experience. It simply says, as within, so without: your outer life will tend to be a mirror image of your inner life. Your external world will tend to correspond almost exactly to what is going on inside both your conscious and subconscious minds.

Your outer life will tend to be a mirror image of your inner life.

There are four major areas where you see the law of correspondence working all the time. The first is simply in your attitude. Often even before you even say anything, people will reflect your attitude back to you in the way they talk to you and treat you: as within, so without.

The second area where the law of correspondence is evident is in your relationships, which will almost perfectly mirror your attitude and personality. If you're a good and happy person, you'll have good and happy relationships. As you become more patient, tolerant, and loving, your relationships will reflect this fact almost immediately, like a mirror.

The third area of correspondence is in your health. Much of your health can be directly traced to specific attitudes that cause you to suffer from minor and major illnesses. The extensive work that's been done in holistic medicine suggests that there are corresponding attitudes of mind for most illnesses, from the common cold and flu all the way up to the most serious, life-threatening illnesses. Whenever you're anxious, upset, or unhappy for any period of time, your body will begin to reflect those feelings. The entire basis of psychosomatic medicine is the conclusion that your mind—*psyche*—makes your body—*soma*—sick. What your mind harbors, your body eventually expresses.

The fourth application of the law of correspondence is that your external world of material accomplishment will exactly correspond to your internal world of preparation. The more knowledge and skill you gain that helps you to be more effective in your work, the more you will be paid. You can't hope to acquire or achieve anything more on the outside than you've acquired or achieved it on the inside. The law of correspondence reigns supreme.

The Law of Belief

The fifth law of success is the *law of belief,* which says that whatever you believe with emotion becomes your reality. You tend to act in a manner consistent with your innermost beliefs and convictions. Your beliefs act like a filter or a screen that edit out incoming information: they only allow into your conscious awareness the things that you've already decided are true about yourself and the world. The great psychologist William James said that belief creates the actual fact. The Bible says that as a man thinketh in his heart, so is he. For example, if you absolutely believe that you are meant to be a great success in life and that no matter what happens, nothing can stop you from achieving greatness, you'll act in a manner consistent with that belief and eventually make it come true. Conversely, if you doubt your ability to be successful for any reason, you will reflect this negative belief in a tendency to hold yourself back.

The most important part of the law of belief is the necessity for questioning your self-limiting beliefs, which act like brakes on your potential. These are the nagging doubts and fears that people have about themselves and their abilities that cause them to sell themselves short. When you have self-limiting beliefs, you tend to settle for far less than you may be capable of.

Self-limiting beliefs may revolve around your ability to lose weight, quit smoking, earn a certain amount of money, be attractive to members of the opposite sex, or develop new abilities that are more conducive to your success and happiness.

One of the most important steps you can take toward success is to question these self-limiting beliefs. You might even ask others who know you well what self-limiting beliefs they think you have that may be holding you back.

Self-limiting beliefs are often used as excuses. A good way to test your self-limiting beliefs is to ask yourself whether anyone else with the limitations you perceive you have has nonetheless gone on to achieve success. If anyone else has been able to overcome these limitations, you can probably overcome them as well. When you think about it, you'll realize almost immediately that hundreds, perhaps thousands, of men and women have had it far worse than you have, yet have gone on to accomplish great things. You begin to fly when you let go of your self-limiting beliefs and allow your mind and aspirations to rise to greater heights.

The Law of Values

The sixth law of success is the *law of values*. The law of values says that what you truly value and believe is only and always expressed in your actions. You can tell the true values of others by looking at what they do, not at what they say. You can also look at your own actions to decide what you truly value. It's not what you say or hope or wish or intend that truly expresses your values and beliefs; it's only what you do. Children are very aware of this and they ignore the advice of their parents when their parents say, "Do as I say, not as I do." We all seem to know that a person's actions are the true reflection of their innermost convictions.

There's a great deal of confusion and unhappiness in the world today because many people feel that if they say or write about something emphatically enough, it means that they truly believe it, but this is false. You only truly believe what you do. Your actions do speak far more loudly than your words. For example, if you truly believe in the values of persistence and dedication, it'll be evident in the things that you do every single day. If you truly believe in honesty, integrity, and self-discipline, you'll demonstrate these qualities in your every behavior.

In fact, you can tell what a person values by looking at what they did in the past when the pressure was on. Only when you're forced to make a choice do you know what you really value. For example, when you have to choose between family and work or between money and honesty, your true values come out.

The wonderful thing about your values is that you can develop them by disciplining yourself to act consistently with them, even if you haven't yet made them a fixed part of your character.

The Law of Motivation

The seventh law of success is the *law of motivation*. Everything you do is triggered by inner desires, urges, and instincts, many of which may be unconscious. Your attitudes and behavior will be determined by your dominant motivations, by what you really want and need, not by what you think you want. This is an extension of the law of values.

There's a formula called the *ABC formula* of human motivation and human action. *ABC* stands for *antecedents, behavior*, and *consequences*. The antecedents are the things that happen before the behavior. The behaviors are the things you do. The consequences are what happen as a result of your behavior.

We know that psychologically only about 15 percent of your motivation comes from the antecedents: from what you read or learn or are told to do or not do. About 85 percent of your motivation comes from your expectations: what you think will happen.

Your beliefs about the consequences, about the future, cause you to behave in a certain way. The clearer you are about the consequences of your actions and the more intensely you desire to enjoy the consequences that your behaviors may lead to, the more motivated you'll be. This is why it's so important to have absolute clarity with regard to your goals in order to perform at your very best.

An important point with regard to the ABC formula is that your behaviors are not guaranteed to achieve the consequences that you desire, but every behavior or action that you engage in will generate a consequence of some kind. Moreover, both actions and inaction have consequences. What you do as well as what you fail to do will have consequences in your future, some of which can be dramatic and long-lasting.

A good exercise is to write out a description of the type of person that you'd like to be and the kind of life that you'd like to be living. The most powerful faculty that you have is your ability to think, your ability to understand. The more accurately you can think about who you are, what you want to accomplish, and how to accomplish it, the more effective and successful you will be.

The Law of Subconscious Activity

The eighth law of success is the *law of subconscious activity*, and it has several applications. The first part of this law is that whatever thought or idea that you hold in your conscious mind, mixed with emotion, will be accepted as a command by your subconscious mind. Hence you can attain whatever thought, idea, or goal you can hold in your mind on a continuing basis, because your subconscious mind will go to work to organize your thoughts and actions to bring it into your reality. If you desire to earn or attain a certain amount of money and you think about it continually, day and night, and use every means possible to drive this desire deep into your subconscious mind, your subconscious mind will commit more and more of its reserve capacity toward bringing that goal or desire into your life.

Whatever thought or idea that you hold in your conscious mind, mixed with emotion, will be accepted as a command by your subconscious mind.

The second part of the law of subconscious activity is that your subconscious mind, once you give it the proper commands, will trigger your reticular cortex. Your reticular cortex, aka the reticular activating system, is a small, finger-like part of your brain that alerts you to events and circumstances around you that are consistent with your dominant desires or concerns. For example, if you decided that you wanted to buy a red sports car, this desire would signal to your reticular cortex that red sports cars are now of paramount importance to you. From that moment on, you would see red sports cars everywhere, even a block away. You would become extremely alert and sensitive to red sports cars, as well as to the means of attaining.

If your goal is to achieve financial independence and you imbue this goal with intense desire, your reticular cortex will cause you to be extremely sensitive to opportunities around you that will help you to earn more money. You will hear and see things everywhere that will help you attain this goal. You might have been completely unaware of these things unless you had planted this goal in your subconscious mind.

The third part of the law of subconscious activity is that your subconscious mind, which controls your autonomic nervous system and your muscles, nerves, actions, and reactions, also controls your body language and your tone of voice. One expert concluded that when you fully communicate with others, 55 percent of your message is contained in your body language, 38 percent is in your tone of voice, and only 7 percent is contained in the words you use.

Furthermore, your body language and tone of voice are largely controlled by messages about yourself that you've sent to your subconscious mind. Your subconscious mind will accept your predominant emotional thoughts and organize your entire body, voice, and tone to fit a pattern consistent with them. For example, when you've had a success, you send a charge of emotional energy to your subconscious mind that tells it that you are a winner. For some time afterwards, you walk, talk, act, and think like a winner. Your step will be brisker, your voice will be stronger, your eyes will be more focused, and your body language will display this belief about yourself.

The Law of Expectations

The ninth law of success is the *law of expectations*. It's often called the law of the self-fulfilling prophecy. It's one of the most powerful of all laws because of its simplicity and predictability. This law simply says that whatever you expect with confidence will tend to materialize in your life. You get not what you want but what you expect with the greatest intensity. For this reason, an attitude of positive self-expectancy seems to go hand in hand with great success.

The wonderful thing about this law is that you have the power to manufacture your own expectations. You can decide to expect only good things to happen to you. You can walk, talk, and act as though you believe the entire world was conspiring to help you to achieve your goals.

You can become what insurance magnate W. Clement Stone called an "inverse paranoid": you can become convinced that the entire world is conspiring to do you good. You apply this law by confidently looking for the good in every person and every situation. You can even look into setbacks for the valuable lessons they might contain. Instead of becoming upset, you can say to yourself, "I believe in the perfect outcome of every situation in my life." This kind of affirmation causes you to approach everything you do with a more positive, open, and optimistic attitude.

The most powerful expectations are those you have of yourself. You should approach everything you do with an attitude of calm, confident self-expectancy. Expect to be successful more times than you're unsuccessful. Expect to win more times than you lose, and expect to eventually achieve your goals if you carry on long enough.

The Law of Concentration

The tenth law of success, which applies to many other areas of life, is called the *law of concentration*: whatever you concentrate on and think about repeatedly and with emotion tends to become a part of your inner and outer life.

Research in psychology shows that if you dwell upon qualities that you wish to develop, like courage, sincerity, and persistence, you tend to build those qualities, brick by brick, into your character and personality.

The law of concentration goes hand in hand with the law of subconscious activity, and it largely explains the person that you are today. Whatever you've concentrated on in the past and are concentrating on in the present is having a major impact on your conduct and behavior. What you concentrate on largely determines the quality and quantity of the results that you get and the success that you enjoy.

The Law of Habit

The eleventh law of success is the *law of habit*: virtually everything that you do is automatic and unthinking. You are largely a creature of habit. From the time you get up in the morning to the time you go to bed at night, you tend to follow the path of least resistance and do the things that you've become accustomed to doing in the past. You eat the same foods for breakfast. You brush your teeth with the same toothpaste; you take the same route to work. You greet people with the same words. You go to lunch at the same time; you work in the same way.

Now there's nothing wrong with establishing habits that enable you to simplify your life. In fact, your life becomes successful to the degree to which many of the things you once needed to concentrate on, such as driving a car, have become automatic and unthinking. When you make certain activities habitual so they no longer require thought, your mind becomes free to concentrate on other things that can be more helpful for achieving the things that you really want.

Good habits are hard to form, but easy to live with. Conversely, bad habits are easy to form but hard to live with. Bad habits are difficult to change. But because they are counterproductive to your goals, it's important to analyze and think through your habits. You need to decide whether or not they are moving you towards your goals or away from them.

Everything you do moves you in one direction or in the other. Nothing is neutral. Everything counts. If a habit isn't helpful, it is hurtful. If a habit is not leading you to success, it's probably leading you to failure.

You overcome bad habits simply by overriding them with the development of new, more positive habits. For example, if you have a golf swing that's causing your ball to go into the rough, you can override it by taking lessons and learning how to hit the ball differently. If you have a habit of getting up later than you should, you can override it by repeatedly getting up earlier until that new behavior becomes the habit.

By practicing the law of concentration in conjunction with the law of habit and thinking continually about how you would be with a new habit or behavior, you drive this message into your subconscious mind, and you eventually begin to behave in a manner consistent with the new habits you wish to form.

The Law of Attraction

This brings us to the twelfth law, one of the most important of all the laws of success: *the law of attraction*. The law of attraction says that you are a living magnet: you inevitably attract into your life the people, events, and circumstances that harmonize with your dominant thoughts.

You attract into your life the people, events, and circumstances that harmonize with your dominant thoughts.

This is why we say that whatever you can hold in your mind on a continuing basis, you can have. Whatever thought you hold clearly and mix with emotion begins to set up a force field of mental energy that draws towards you the things that you need to achieve that goal.

This law of attraction has been written about for hundreds if not thousands of years. It's contained in the folk sayings "Like attracts like," or "Like begets like," or perhaps you've heard that birds of a feather flock together. My friend Mark Victor Hansen, coauthor of the Chicken Soup for the Soul book series, says that whatever you want wants you. These are all ways of saying that your mind is extremely powerful; whatever you think emotionalized becomes a form of energy, like a magnet that's attracting events and circumstances into your life.

In music, the law of attraction is often called the law of sympathetic resonance. For example, if you have two pianos in a large room and you hit the key of C on one and walk across the room to the other one, the C note on the second piano will be vibrating in perfect resonance with the one on the first.

One common example of this law is when you enter a room full of people and you almost invariably feel a sympathetic resonance with someone else in the room. You'll gravitate toward a person with whom you are comfortable and compatible, and that person will gravitate towards you. Often two single people at a social gathering will have a sympathetic resonance that draws them toward each other. By the same token, when you have a clear goal or idea, you'll attract and be attracted to people who have ideas, information, and resources that can help you to realize that goal.

Another illustration of the law of attraction is its opposite: the law of repulsion. When you begin to become a particular kind of person, you'll find yourself attracted to people who are similar to you; you will also find yourself repelling and being repelled by people who don't think the way you do. This law explains why positive people tend to associate with other positive people and why negative people tend to associate with other negative people, and why neither group finds the other group of very much interest. You can fill your life with the kind of people that you respect and admire by simply becoming the kind of person in your thoughts that will attract them to you.

The Law of Choice

The thirteenth law of success is the *law of choice*, which says that you are always free to choose the content of your conscious mind, but in so doing, you are choosing every other part of your life. Your thoughts control your reality. Since no one else can think for you, the thoughts that you choose to harbor determine everything that happens in your life.

The wonderful thing about the law of choice is that it says that you have complete freedom to think and therefore to be anything that you intensely desire. The choice is always up to you. You are where you are and what you are because you have chosen to be there. If you're not happy with where you are and what you are, it's up to you to choose to be and do something else.

The Law of Optimism

The fourteenth law of success is the *law of optimism*, which says that a positive mental attitude goes hand in hand with success and happiness in virtually every dimension of life. Optimism makes you into a cheerful and pleasant person, a person that other people like and want to be around and help. The most successful men and women tend to be very likable people. The more optimistic you are, the happier you'll be moment to moment, and the more things you'll be willing to attempt.

The Law of Change

The fifteenth law of success, *the law of change*, says that change is inevitable. Change is the only constant in life. Everything is changing even as you read this book, but the wonderful thing is that nothing is fixed either. All progress requires change. Since change is happening in any case, you can be, have, and do anything you want by simply harnessing the forces of change. Your life can only get better when you get better. You can't remain the same and somehow improve. If you don't take advantage of change, you will end up being its victim. Things will happen over which you have little or no control, and you'll have to adjust your actions and behaviors to whatever occurs.

The Laws in Practice

Now let me tell you a story that is true in more cases than not. Once upon a time there was a young man from an average home with an average education, working at an average job and with an average group of friends. Like most average young men, he was primarily interested in girls, sports, and television. He liked to have a good time, and he spent most of his money enjoying himself. He looked upon his job as a necessary evil that paid for his average lifestyle, and like most average people, he was going nowhere with his life.

Then one day something happened to him. Perhaps he read a book that woke him up or listened to an audio program or attended a motivational seminar. Whatever it was, he wasn't the same afterwards. He realized that he could choose to do and be something else. He applied the law of choice. By the law of change, he realized that his life could only improve if he began changing in a positive direction. Using the law of cause and effect, he made some decisions about what he wanted to accomplish and began searching out the causes of the effects he desired. Using the law of optimism, he was positive about himself and his possibilities. He expected good things to happen, triggering the law of expectation. He went to work on his thinking, and he began to use the law of concentration on his ideal lifestyle.

By the law of subconscious activity, he began to walk and talk like the person he envisioned himself becoming. He also began noticing opportunities to advance himself that he hadn't seen before. As he changed his thinking, he triggered the law of mind and the law of mental equivalency, and he created a clear picture of his goals. By the law of correspondence, his outer world began to reflect his new, improved inner world. His beliefs about himself began to change, and by the law of attraction, people and resources began to appear to help him move toward his goal. As he concentrated on his desires, his values and motivations changed, and he began developing the kind of habits that lead to success. By bringing his life into alignment with the laws of success, he began moving forward at a rate that surprised even him, and so can you.

The laws of success are based on the foundational principle that in order to succeed, you must first decide what success means to you. You can then begin to apply these laws to bring your definition of success more rapidly into your reality. There are no limitations on what you can be, have, or do except those you place on your own mind. When you begin to live your life and guide your thinking consistently with the laws that we've just described, you'll begin to experience successes that are beyond anything that you might have imagined. You can accomplish more in a year or two than many people accomplish in five or even ten years. When you practice the laws of success, your future can be unlimited.

The Laws of Success

The law of cause and effect. For every effect, there is a cause or a series of causes.

The law of mind. Thoughts objectify themselves; thoughts held in mind produce after their kind.

The law of mental equivalency. Your primary responsibility to yourself is to create a clear and accurate mental equivalent of what you wish to experience in your external life.

The law of correspondence. As within, so without. Your outer life will tend to be a mirror image of your inner life.

The law of belief. Whatever you believe with emotion becomes your reality.

The law of values. What you truly value and believe is only and always expressed in your actions.

The law of motivation. Everything you do is triggered by inner desires, urges, and instincts, many of which may be unconscious. Your attitudes and behavior will be determined by your dominant motivations, by what you really want and need, not by what you think you want.

The law of subconscious activity. Whatever thought or idea that you hold in your conscious mind, mixed with emotion, will be accepted as a command by your subconscious mind.

The law of expectation. Whatever you expect with confidence will tend to materialize in your life. You get not what you want but what you expect with the greatest intensity.

The law of concentration. Whatever you concentrate on and think about repeatedly and with emotion tends to become a part of your inner and outer life.

The law of habit. Virtually everything that you do is automatic and unthinking. You are largely a creature of habit. You tend to follow the path of least resistance and to do the things that you've become accustomed to doing in the past.

The law of attraction. You inevitably attract into your life the people, events, and circumstances that harmonize with your dominant thoughts.

The law of choice. You are always free to choose the content of your conscious mind, but in so doing, you are choosing every other part of your life. Your thoughts control your reality.

The law of optimism. A positive mental attitude goes hand in hand with success and happiness.

The law of change. Change is inevitable. Change is the only constant in life.

two

The Laws of Achievement

In the previous chapter, I talked about the laws of success. In this chapter, I'll be talking about the laws of achievement and how you can use them to go further and faster than you ever dreamed possible.

You might be wondering about the difference between the two. They sound the same, and in many respects, they are. Success and achievement are the flip sides of the same coin. They're similar but different in design and purpose.

Success can be defined as wanting what you get. Success is not necessarily determined by material things or accomplishments. You can enjoy it simply by reaching the point where you are perfectly content with your life in every respect and you feel no dissatisfaction or pressing need for anything else. In this sense, you can be a success sitting by yourself in a quiet place, contemplating the world.

Achievement is considerably different. It refers to getting what you want rather than wanting what you get. Achievement means the ability to set goals and objectives, make plans of action, implement those plans, overcome obstacles and adversity, and achieve the ends that you set for yourself.

In addition to the laws of success, there are a series of laws that are specific to goal attainment. These are the laws that I'll describe in this chapter. The basic rule of human action is that everything you do is aimed at improving your life in some way. Every action of yours is guided by purpose and intention of some kind, whether clear or unclear.

Start with Goals

The remarkable thing about your mind and your abilities is that you always seem to achieve the goals that you set for yourself. If your goal is a small one, for example, to get home at night and watch television, you'll certainly achieve it. If your goal is a large one—to achieve financial success, prosperity, and prestige—you'll achieve that as well. Your mind contains a cybernetic goal-seeking function. Once you've programmed an intense desire into your subconscious mind, your subconscious and your superconscious minds take on a power of their own, which seems to drive you inevitably toward the attainment of your ideal. In this sense, goal achieving seems to happen almost automatically.

The problem is always the setting of clear goals and the harnessing of your mental and physical energy behind those goals. When you learn to do that, the rest seems to happen with an almost irresistible inevitability. As I said in the previous chapter, the application of these laws begins with becoming perfectly clear about your ideal desired result or purpose. You need to determine where you want to end up. Just as you wouldn't go to the grocery store without a shopping list, you wouldn't think of living your life without a clear list of the things that you wish to attain and a written plan of action for attaining them.

Unfortunately, according to virtually every study, less than 3 percent of adult Americans have clear written goals or detailed plans. According to Mark McCormack in his book *What They Still Don't Teach You at the Harvard Business School*, people with written goals accomplished ten times as much in the same period of time as those with no written goal.

You can move into the top rank of Americans living today by the simple act of sitting down with a pad of paper and a pen and writing out where you intend to go and what you intend to do to get there over the next three to five years. You'll immediately become a different person, and your chances of accomplishing what you have written down will go up by about 1000 percent.

In my seminars, I continually urge people to write down ten things that they want to achieve in the next twelve months. I tell them that if they do this, at the end of twelve months they can reread the list and they will find that probably eight of those ten items have been achieved, sometimes in the most remarkable ways.

Countless graduates from my seminars tell me this is exactly what happens. For example, an insurance executive from Houston took this recommendation from me at a seminar on a Thursday afternoon. The following Sunday, he sat down and made a list of ten things he wanted to accomplish within the next twelve months. The following evening, Monday, he opened the list and found to his astonishment that he had already accomplished five of his ten one-year goals. He quickly wrote down five more goals, bringing his list back up to ten, and by the following Thursday evening, he had accomplished five more of the new list. He had achieved more in five days with written goals than he had expected to accomplish in twelve months of hard work.

The Law of Control

Aside from clarity regarding your goals, there are twelve laws you need to know and practice if you really aspire to high achievement.

The first, and one of the most important laws that you'll ever learn, is the *law of control*. It simply says that you feel positive about yourself to the degree to which you feel you are in control of your own life.

You feel positive about yourself to the degree to which you feel you are in control of your own life.

Psychologists have long acknowledged the importance of control for human personality and performance. They have concluded that a sense of control is essential to perform at your best. They use the term *locus of control*, which refers to where you feel the control is in any particular part of your life. If you feel that you are self-determined and you determine the direction of your activities, you are considered to have an *internal locus of control*. If you feel that you are controlled by your boss, your bills, your childhood experiences, your health, or anything else, you are considered to have an *external locus of control*.

This locus of control is the critical element in health and well-being. People with an internal locus of control—those who feel that they are behind the wheel of their own lives—tend to be low-stress, high-performance personalities. On the other hand, those with an external locus of control—those who feel that what they're doing is determined by other people and pressures—have a high level of stress and a commensurately low level of performance.

The first part of the law of control is the same as the law of change, which says that change is inevitable. Change is also scary for most people: most people have a deep-rooted desire to avoid change of any kind, even positive change. But having goals allows you to control the direction of change and ensure that it goes predominantly in the direction that you desire. Goals give you control over the critical elements of your life. Without them, you are driving down the highway of life with your hands off the wheel.

The second part of the law of control is that controlled change tends to lead inevitably to greater achievement than uncontrolled change. The habit of working toward accomplishing important goals on a daily basis will ensure that you'll achieve at a far higher level than if you had no goals at all.

The third part of the law is that to take control of your life, you must begin by taking control of your mind. Your ability to think the thoughts you want and determine the goals and results you desire is the starting point of happiness and high attainment.

Many people believe that life is a series of random occurrences and that things just happen by accident. They don't realize that by failing to plan, they're planning to fail. Nobody actually plans to live a life of underachievement and frustration, but by failing to decide specifically what they want, they end up living unconsciously and unintentionally. Consequently, their lives will appear to be a series of random occurrences over which they have little control.

People who believe they have little control over their lives say things like, "You can't fight city hall," or "it's not what you know, it's *who* you know," or "it's a matter of being in the right place at the right time." Many of these people believe that success is largely due to luck and contacts and has very little to do with themselves. In a recent survey, 63 percent of adult Americans revealed that they believed that the only way they were going to achieve financial independence was to win a lottery of some kind. This means that the great majority of people think their lives are simply one big crapshoot over which they can exert little control. People who live by this philosophy—which is contrary to the law of cause and effect and the law of control—have a perceived lack of control, so they experience negativity, pessimism, helplessness, and a feeling of victimhood.

People who fail to plan their lives tend to blame others for their problems. They continually make excuses for performing well below their potential and indulge in forms of escapism such as endless television watching, alcohol, drugs, and aimless socializing. They don't feel that they can make much of a difference.

The very act of setting goals enables you to escape from the clutches of randomness and put yourself squarely under the laws of control and cause and effect. Goal setting gives you a feeling of power, purpose, and forward direction. It puts you in charge of your life and makes you feel terrific about yourself. This is why we call goal setting the master skill of success. It is more important to your overall happiness and well-being than any other single skill that you can develop.

The Law of Responsibility

The second law of achievement is the *law of responsibility*. This law says that you are completely responsible for everything you are and have and everything you become and achieve.

The concept of individual responsibility is a major issue in society today. There are basically two schools of thought on this issue. One school believes that no one is really responsible and that the government or society is to blame for anything unfortunate that happens to anyone. The other school of thought says that in a society of individual freedom, individual responsibility is essential and that people are responsible for the consequences of what they do or neglect to do.

Responsibility is not optional; it's mandatory. No further progress is possible except to the degree to which you assert a higher level of responsibility in a given area. No one else can or will do it for you. Curiously, the more responsibility you accept, the more people will want to help you; the less responsibility that you accept, the less people will want to have anything to do with you.

The first aspect of the law of responsibility is that since you are always free to choose what you think and do, you are where you are and what you are because of your own conduct and behavior. Because you have complete freedom of choice and can do and say anything you want, you can never evade complete responsibility for what you do or fail to do.

The second part of this law is that responsibility begins with taking full and complete control over the content of your conscious mind and your dominant thoughts. As we've seen, what you think determines your reality. Since only you can control what you think, the very act of seizing control of your thoughts and keeping them on what you want and off what you don't want is the beginning of self-mastery, self-control, and self-responsibility.

The third part of the law of responsibility is simply that no one is coming to the rescue. If it's to be, it's up to you. If anything is going to get better in your life, it is only because *you* get better. If anything's going to change, it's only because *you* change. If things are going to improve, it is because *you* improve.

Accepting complete responsibility for who you are and everything you become gives you a tremendous sense of control and freedom. It makes you feel positive and happy about yourself. It puts you under the high road to effective achievement. It enables you to put your foot on the accelerator of your own potential and to move more rapidly toward the accomplishment of the things that are important to you.

The Dream List

This brings us to the necessity of deciding exactly what you want in life. Here are some simple exercises that you can follow. Your first job is to make a dream list: a list of everything that you could ever want to have or be or do, written as though you have no limitations whatsoever on your potential. Imagine for the moment that you have no limitations with regard to your ability or your education. Imagine you have no limitations with regard to resources or contacts. Imagine that you have no limitations with regard to your intelligence, skills, or abilities. Imagine that you have no limitations with regard to time, money, or other constraints.

Just let your mind run freely, and for a few minutes write down everything that you could think of that you would like to accomplish in the next one to five or ten years or beyond. The key is not to allow self-limiting beliefs, fears, and doubts to creep in and sabotage this exercise. The poor performer naturally tends to be thinking about the reason why things are not possible rather than defining clearly what he or she wants in advance of taking those limitations into consideration. Some people will come up with a list of five or ten things they want. Others will come up with 200 or 300 items.

One very successful real estate broker, a friend of mine, started off by writing down everything he could possibly want in a spiral notebook. Over time, he filled many pages with hundreds of small and large goals. Eventually he became extraordinarily successful and made an enormous amount of money, with which he was able to achieve most of the goals he'd written down.

Goals are the fuel in the furnace of achievement. This goes back to the law of motivation, which says that in order for there to be motivation, there must be a motive. Eighty-five percent of your motivation is determined by the consequences that you anticipate or the things that you hope to achieve as a result of certain actions and behaviors. The clearer you are about what you want and the more things you want, the more motivated and energetic you'll be in obtaining them.

Goals are the fuel in the furnace of achievement.

Once you've written down everything you can think of, set priorities on your goals. Go back over the list and write down an A, B, or C next to each item. Next to the items that are most important to you—the ones that can make the greatest difference in your life and which you desire most intensely—write the letter A. Next to the things that you would like to have but which are not as important as the first category, write the letter B. Next to each of the remaining items—things that would be nice for you to accomplish but which you don't care passionately about—write the letter C.

The second part of this exercise is to transfer all of your A goals to a separate sheet of paper. Once you've done this, go back over these goals and organize them by writing A1 next to the most important goal, A2 next to the second most important goal, A3 next to the third most important goal, and so on until you've organized all of your A goals in order of importance to you. Your A1 goal should be your major definite purpose: the most important single goal in your life. Successful men and women have goals in each important part of their lives, but they also have one goal, which is their umbrella goal, the single most important thing they are working on at any given time.

It's also advisable to divide your goals into three categories of another type. The first category is your personal and family goals. These are *why* you're doing what you're doing. It's very important for you to be crystal clear about the underlying reasons why you want the tangible goals that you're working for. Many people get sidetracked working for material things and lose all sight of why they're doing it.

Your second set of goals is your career and material goals. These are the *what* of your goal list. They are the things that you have to do in order to get to the *why*. Goals of this kind will include career achievements, financial income, quantities of sales or profits.

The third category consists of development goals. These are the *how* goals: the things that you must do or become competent at doing in order to achieve the material goals, which in turn will lead you to the accomplishment of your personal goals. You need to have a set of goals in each of these areas for your life to be in balance and to perform at your very best.

The Planning Stage

The next step is to begin the planning stage. Here you take a clean sheet of paper and write your A1 goal at the top of the page in the present tense, as though it were already a reality. For example, you could write, "I earn $200,000 per year."

Now use the twenty-idea method. Write down a list of twenty things that you could do that would help you move toward that goal. Write down everything you can think of, for example, "I could work harder and smarter in my current field and increase my productivity and income." Or "I could upgrade my skills so that the value of my work is higher for the same number of hours." You could also write something completely different, such as, "I could change my career or company completely and start at a different job or in a different industry."

In any case, write down at least twenty activities that would help you to achieve your goals. Once you've done that, do the same thing for each of your other A goals, so that you have a series of A goals with a list of twenty activities or more that you could engage in to accomplish each one.

Now take your first list of twenty items under your A1 goal, and organize those items by time and priority. Which things can you or should you do first? What things are most important and would make the greatest difference to the attainment of the goal? Write down an A, B, or C next to each of the twenty items. Then write down A1, A2, A3, B1, B2, B3, and so on next to the items so that you have organized them from beginning to end.

You now have a list of your most important goals organized by priority and a list of the activities you must engage in to achieve those goals, also organized by priority. Your final exercise is to merge your major goals and your major activities into a single plan and organize your day-to-day life around that plan.

Review this plan on a regular basis. Resolve to do something every day to move yourself toward one of your most important goals. This will help you to develop and maintain momentum. You'll be astonished at how rapidly you make progress on even the largest and most challenging goals using this method.

The Law of Compensation

The third law of achievement is the *law of compensation*: you are always fully compensated for whatever you do. It's often called the *law of reciprocity*, which says that people will always reciprocate in kind for whatever you do either to or for them.

My late friend Zig Ziglar, the great speaker and motivator, formulated what we might call Ziglar's law, which is a corollary of the law of compensation. It says you can have anything you want in life if you just help enough other people get what they want.

The law of compensation is a sublaw of the law of cause and effect or the law of sowing and reaping, which says, with the Bible, that whatsoever a man soweth, that also shall he reap. The law of compensation says that whatever you put in you get out. You cannot reap it unless you have sown in it in advance.

In fact, whatever you're reaping today is a measure of what you've sown in the past. If you want to reap something more in the future, you have to sow something more or different or better in the present. It's completely up to you.

In his wonderful essay "Compensation," which is one of the finest pieces of writing in the English language, Ralph Waldo Emerson says that the longer you put in without getting out, the greater will be your return when it finally comes. Years ago, the Kingston Trio had a song that said, "You've got to prime the pump, you must have faith and believe / You've got to give of yourself 'fore you're worthy to receive." This principle runs throughout all of human history and is virtually inviolate.

The Law of Service

This leads us to the fourth law of achievement: the *law of service*, which says that your rewards in life will always be in direct proportion to the value of your service to others.

The first part of this law is that all fortunes begin with the sale of personal services. The second part says that if you wish to increase the size of your rewards, you must increase the quality and quantity of your service. The third part says that everyone works on commission.

In his book *In Search of Excellence*, Tom Peters says that the top managers in the leading companies all seem to be obsessed with customer service. The most successful men and women are those who are able to lose themselves in serving the people who depend upon them—their customers, employers, and others.

When you combine the laws of compensation and service, you have the key to obtaining anything that you really want. You'll get out exactly what you put in, and wonderfully, you have complete control over what you put in. When you devote yourself completely to serving your customers, your boss, your staff, and the people who purchase or use your products and services, it gives you a tremendous feeling of meaning and purpose. It causes you to feel that you are really making a difference in the world.

In his book *The Making of an Achiever*, Alan Cox says that the most successful people in any corporation are those who are able to lose themselves in their jobs and in serving their customers. When you throw your whole heart into making your customers happy and serving them better than anyone else, you'll be putting both your career and your financial life onto the fast track.

One key to mental and emotional well-being is to know that you are working at the outside limit of your potential. You need to feel that you're stretching yourself fully and that you're putting your whole heart into what you're doing.

The Law of Applied Effort

The fifth law of achievement is the *law of applied effort*. This law simply says that all things are amenable to hard work. Nothing will bring you to the attention of your superiors faster than developing a reputation for being a hard worker. People who are in a position to help you and accelerate your career tend to be impressed by your willingness to work harder and longer than anyone else. In Dr. Thomas Stanley's study of affluent Americans, almost every one of the self-made millionaires he interviewed told him that their success was due more to hard work than to any other factor.

In America, you work forty hours per week for survival. If all you work is forty hours, all you get is enough money to survive. You tread water and you stay even, but you don't get very far ahead, and you never achieve the kind of success that's possible for you. However, every hour over forty hours that you put in, either on your job or on yourself, improving your knowledge and skills, is an investment in your success. You can tell where you're going to be in three to five years simply by looking at the number of hours over forty that you are working each week.

The average work week for both executives and small business owners in America is approximately fifty-eight to fifty-nine hours.

Many successful men and women work seventy and even eighty hours a week during the critical formative stages of their careers.

Furthermore, all great success is preceded by a long period of hard work in a single direction toward a clearly defined purpose. Continually ask yourself, what am I trying to do and how am I trying to do it? It's not enough just to work hard or to work long hours. You must be working on high value-added tasks and activities toward the accomplishment of meaningful and important goals.

A second part of this law is that the harder you work, the luckier you get. Your ability to work hard will open up the Red Sea of opportunity for you and will bring to your assistance all manner of people and resources that you could not have imagined.

The third part of the law of applied effort says that to achieve more than the average, you must work longer and harder than the average. This is simply a way of restating the fact that you can only take more out of life if you're putting more into life, and the more you put in, the more you'll get out. The law of cause and effect is absolute. You will invariably reap what you sow, and if you sow more, you'll eventually reap more.

The Law of Overcompensation

The sixth law of achievement is the *law of overcompensation*. This is a companion law to the law of applied effort, and it simply says that you must continually look for opportunities to go beyond the requirements of your job. Napoleon Hill, perhaps the foremost researcher on success in the first half of the twentieth century, concluded that one of the keys to great success in America was the willingness to go the extra mile. Your future potential is unlimited, because there's no restriction on the extra ways you can add greater value to your work.

One of the keys to great success is the willingness to go the extra mile.

You can go the extra mile in everything you do. Every day and in every way, you can always look for opportunities to exceed expectations. Inspirational speaker Earl Nightingale advised that you should always put in more than you take out, or you'll never take out more than you're getting right now. The only way that you can be paid more is by putting greater value into your work and achieving greater results. Another way of stating the law of over-compensation is that you must always do more than you're paid for if you ever want to be paid for more than you're doing.

Some decades ago, a young woman who was working as a secretary for a large company in Florida came to me at a seminar and told me her story. She said that she had listened to one of my audios and as a result had set a goal to increase her income by 50 percent. In her heart she didn't really believe this was possible because of the salary structure in her company. Nonetheless, she went to work to increase the value of her service to her boss. She applied the law of overcompensation to everything she did. She learned how to do new things; she began a little earlier and stayed a little later. Within six months, her boss had quietly raised her salary in stages from $1,500 per month to $2,250 per month and had given her these increases without her ever having asked for them. All she did was to concentrate on seeking out ways to work harder and smarter and to serve her boss better with the things he needed. He automatically increased her pay because he recognized how much she had increased her value to him. She worked up to the age of twenty-five to get her salary up to $1,500 per month. In just six months, however, by applying these principles, she increased her salary by 50 percent, and so can you. It is simply a matter of applying these laws to your work on a daily basis.

The Law of Preparation

The seventh law of achievement is the *law of preparation*, which says that perfect performance is preceded by painstaking preparation. The serious person, the real professional in any field, takes more time to prepare thoroughly than the average person. The nonserious person or the nonprofessional always attempts to bluff or wing it. They try to get by with a minimum of preparation without realizing that their level of preparation is immediately evident to everyone around them.

One of my favorite quotes, which has had a powerful effect in shaping my life, comes from Abraham Lincoln: "I shall study and prepare myself, and someday my chance will come."

He recognized, as do all great men and women, that painstaking and thorough preparation is the key to the future.

The first part of the law of preparation is simply to do your homework. The details will trip you up every time. My friend Joel Weldon gave a wonderful talk a few years ago entitled "Elephants Don't Bite." The essence of his talk was that it was the mosquitoes of life, the small things that tend to be ignored, that cause you the most trouble. No one ever gets bitten by an elephant, but people get bitten by mosquitoes all the time. His message was that if you want to get to the top of your field, you must be fastidious about the little things, because as a minister once said, "God is in the details."

The second part of the law of preparation comes from the management guru Peter Drucker, who wrote that "action without thinking is the cause of every failure." Action without taking the time to think through the details in their possible ramifications seems to be the underlying cause of most failure. Conversely, action preceded by thinking and planning is the cause of virtually every success. This doesn't mean that you'll automatically succeed if you plan thoroughly in advance, but it means that you must almost inevitably fail if you don't.

The third part of this law says that if it's not worth doing, it's not worth doing well. Details are important, it's true, but you need to think through the value and importance of each detail before you overcommit your time and resources to them.

The Law of Forced Efficiency

The eighth law of achievement is the *law of forced efficiency*. This law states that the more things you have to do in a limited space of time, the more you'll be forced to work on your most important tasks. This is another way of saying that there's never enough time to do everything, but there's always enough time to do the important things. The more you take on, the more likely it is that you'll be forced to evaluate your activities in such a way that you spend your limited mental and physical energy on just those tasks that are the most vital to your success.

There are two parts of the law of forced efficiency. The first is that there will never be enough time to do everything that you have to do. The busier and more successful you become, the truer this statement will be. If you have lots of time to do your work, it means that you are underemployed, underpaid, and well along on the low road to frustration and disappointment in your career.

You can only discover how much you can do by trying to do too much. You can only find out how far you can go by going too far. You discover how much you can take on by taking on more than you can do.

The second part of this law, which is the key question in personal efficiency and time management, is to ask yourself continually, what is the most valuable use of my time right now? Always keep yourself on track and focus on your most important responsibilities by asking yourself hour by hour and minute by minute, what is the most valuable use of my time right now?

The Law of Decision

The ninth law of achievement is the *law of decision*. It says that every great leap forward in life is preceded by a clear decision that leads to action. High-achieving men and women tend to be decisive in their thoughts and actions. They think things through carefully, decide exactly what they want, make clear decisions, and act to make those decisions a reality.

In your life, you've no doubt had several experiences where you've been unsure of what to do and you've resolved your dilemma by making a clear decision one way or the other. In looking back, you'll probably find that that was the turning point for you and that everything else flowed from the decision.

The ability to make good decisions is one of the most critical thinking skills of the successful man or woman. One study compared the careers of managers who were promoted rapidly to those of managers who were passed over for promotion. Researchers found the one distinguishing behavior between the two groups was that the more rapidly promoted managers were more decisive in doing their jobs. Given written tests with hypothetical problems, both sets of managers were equally accurate in their answers. But the more successful managers were willing to make decisions on the job based on those answers while the unsuccessful managers were afraid to act for fear of making a mistake. The very act of being decisive can be the critical factor that enables you to take command of a situation and move ahead more rapidly.

High achievers are not necessarily those who make the right decisions every time, but they are those people who make their decisions right. They accept feedback and self-correct. They take in new information and they change if necessary, but they are always decisive, always moving forward, never wishy-washy or vacillating.

The first part of the law of decision simply says, act boldly and unseen forces will come to your aid. When you grasp a situation and step forward courageously, a series of unseen forces (most of which are explained by the laws in this book) seem to emerge and help you to achieve your goals. Your very willingness to act rather than delay or procrastinate seems to bring universal powers to your assistance.

The second part of the law of decision comes from the wonderful book by Dorothea Brande entitled *Wake Up and Live!* She wrote that the discovery that changed her life and the lives of thousands of others who heard it from her was this simple success formula: act as if it were impossible to fail, and it shall be. When you imagine that your success will be guaranteed if you simply take action and you act on that premise, a whole series of forces begins to support you and move you toward the attainment of your desires. When in doubt, act as if it were impossible to fail, and push forward.

The third part of the law of decision comes from the famous Nike commercial, which says, "Just do it." These three words summarize one of the great formulas for success. Just do it. Be decisive. Go for it. Take a chance. Act boldly, and unseen forces will come to your aid.

The Law of Creativity

The tenth law of achievement is the *law of creativity*. It says that every advance in human life begins with an idea in the mind of one person. The ideas that you generate enable you to solve your problems, overcome your obstacles, and achieve your goals. Ideas are the keys to the future. It's hardly possible to achieve anything of note except to the degree to which you think and do something new and different from what's been done before. All it takes is a small innovation to lay the foundation for a fortune and great success in life.

The first part of this law says that your ability to generate constructive ideas is to all intents and purposes unlimited. Therefore your future potential is unlimited as well. Ideas are a mode of transportation, a vehicle that you can use to take you from wherever you are to wherever you want to go. Your job is simply to generate as many ideas as possible, evaluate them carefully against your current goals, and then act on them. There's virtually no obstacle in life that you cannot overcome with the power of thought, with the power of creative concentration, with the power of ideas.

The second part of this law comes from Napoleon Hill, who famously said, "Whatever the mind of man can conceive and believe, it can achieve." Your mind is structured in such a way that you cannot have an idea without having the ability to bring that idea into reality. The very existence of an idea in your conscious mind means that you have within you and around you the capacity to achieve it. The only question you have to ask yourself is, how badly do I want it?

**Whatever the mind of man can
conceive and believe, it can achieve.**

The third part of the law of creativity comes from Napoleon Bonaparte, who said that imagination rules the world. Everything you see around you is the result of what was initially a single idea in the mind of a single person. Our entire world started from thought, brought into reality.

The fourth and final part of this law comes from Einstein, who said that imagination is more important than facts. On countless occasions in your life, the facts have said one thing, but your ideas and creative energy enabled you to do something completely different. Virtually every important turning point in your life will be marked by an idea that you've had at that time. All great changes in human life and destiny begin with an idea that causes you to see things differently and take action that you would not otherwise have taken. Wherever you are, whatever you're doing, whatever your situation, you have the creative capacity to generate ideas, solve any problem, and achieve any goal. It's up to you.

The Law of Flexibility

The eleventh law of achievement is the *law of flexibility*. This law says that success is best achieved when you are clear about the goal but flexible about the process of attaining it. Flexibility is considered to be perhaps the most important single quality necessary for success in our competitive society.

When you set a clear goal for yourself and make a plan, you usually have a fairly good idea of what you have to do to get what you want. However, a thousand things can change, each of which will require alterations in your plan. The most optimistic and enthusiastic people are open, flexible, and fluid in the face of the inevitable myriad changes required as they move toward accomplishment.

The first part of the law of flexibility says that resistance and frustration often indicate that you're doing the wrong thing. Whenever you feel you're butting your head against the wall and not making progress, step back and reexamine your plan. Be sure the goal that you're working toward is still the goal that you desire, and then sit down and make better plans.

Use the mentality of computer programmers: when they design a program, they know that it will be full of defects when it's completed. No computer program ever works perfectly the first time it's tried. However, the programmer accepts this as a fact of life and later goes back through the program to remove the defects. When the programmer is finished, the program will operate perfectly. By the same token, whenever your plans don't seem to be bearing fruit, look in the mirror and reexamine and redesign your plans until they are faultless and move you forward without frustration.

The second part of the law of flexibility is that you are only as free as the number of developed options that you have available to you. Freedom and happiness are largely determined by the number of alternatives that you've developed in case your first choice doesn't work. The more thoroughly developed your options, the more freedom you have. If one course of action doesn't develop as you expected, you're fully prepared to switch.

In my courses on decision-making, once the decision has been reached, I encourage the participants to ask, what else would be a good decision in this situation? The exercise of developing alternatives enables you to think more clearly and can be a major contributor to your level of achievement.

The third part of the law of flexibility is that crisis is change trying to take place. Whenever you're experiencing a crisis or difficulty, stand back and ask yourself what change is trying to take place here. You may be having a crisis in your work, your relationships, your health, or your business. In almost every case, a crisis indicates that something is wrong and that pursuing the same course would be unwise. So what is the change that's trying to take place in your life right now?

The fourth part of the law of flexibility is that errant assumptions lie at the root of every failure. Almost every failure you have will be based on an incorrect assumption that you've made and accepted without question. It's always a good exercise to clarify your assumptions, especially when things aren't going as well as you want.

What are your assumptions? First, what are your explicit assumptions, the ones you're clearly aware of? Second, what are your implicit assumptions, the ones that you may be accepting without question? What if your most cherished assumptions were wrong? What changes would this dictate? How flexible and fluid would you have to be to redirect your course of action if something that you were assuming as a fact turned out not to be true at all?

You make the right decisions and achieve your goals on schedule because you are operating on assumptions that have turned out to be true. Many people go broke in starting their own businesses because they assume that there's a big enough market for the product or service that they propose to offer. They also assume that customers will switch from their current suppliers to them for no other reason than that they are in the marketplace. They sometimes assume that they have the talents, skills, and abilities to provide the product or service at a competitive price and still make a profit. Your willingness to question your assumptions, test them against reality, and accept that you could be wrong is the attitude that will ultimately lead you to great achievement.

The Law of Persistence

The twelfth law of achievement is the *law of persistence*. It says that your ability to persist in the face of setbacks and disappointments is your measure of your belief in yourself and your ability to succeed. Persistence is the iron quality of success. It may turn out to be your greatest asset. Sometimes the strongest thing you have going for you is your ability to persist longer than anyone else.

The first part of this law simply says that persistence is self-discipline in action. When you persist in spite of the inevitable setbacks and disappointments, you demonstrate to yourself and others that you have the self-discipline and self-mastery that are indispensable for great success.

Winston Churchill summarized the second part of this law when he said, "Never give up. Never, never give up." Churchill believed (and proved throughout his lifetime) that bulldog tenacity in the face of apparently overwhelming defeat was often the critical quality that turned defeat into victory.

When you live your life in harmony with the laws of success and achievement that we've talked about so far, and you back your goals and plans with unshakeable determination and persistence, you will find that nothing in the world can stop you. You will become an irresistible force of nature, and your goals of high achievement will become your realities.

The Laws of Achievement

The law of control. You feel positive about yourself to the degree to which you feel you are in control of your own life.

The law of responsibility. You are completely responsible for everything you are and have and everything you become and achieve.

The law of compensation. You are always fully compensated for what you do.

The law of service. Your rewards will always be in direct proportion to the value of your service to others.

The law of applied effort. All things are amenable to hard work.

The law of overcompensation. You must continually look for opportunities to go beyond the requirements of your job.

The law of preparation. Perfect performance is preceded by painstaking preparation.

The law of forced efficiency. The more things you have to do in a limited time, the more you'll be forced to work on your most important tasks.

The law of decision. Every great leap forward in life is preceded by a clear decision that leads to action. Act boldly, and unseen forces will come to your aid.

The law of creativity. Every advance in human life begins with an idea in the mind of one person.

The law of flexibility. Success is best achieved when you are clear about the goal but flexible about the process of attaining it.

The law of persistence. Your ability to persist in the face of setbacks and disappointments is your measure of your belief in yourself and your ability to succeed.

three

The Laws of Happiness

The Greek philosopher Aristotle wrote that the single most common denominator of humankind is the desire to be happy, however the individual may define happiness. In his *Nicomachean Ethics*, Aristotle wrote that the primary concern of philosophy was to answer the question, how shall we live in order to be happy?

Virtually every action that you take is aimed at somehow achieving your own happiness or moving away from circumstances that cause you to feel unhappy. Sigmund Freud called this the "pleasure principle." For him and for many other psychologists, it became the foundation for studying the mental and emotional aspects of human behavior.

It's safe to say that virtually everything you think or say or do is simply a means for achieving your own happiness. The question of happiness, how to achieve more of it, and how to avoid unhappiness has been studied exhaustively for hundreds of years.

In this chapter, we'll talk about some of the laws that have been discovered in the universal search for happiness. You can then use them to dramatically increase the happiness that you enjoy in virtually everything you do.

The starting point of achieving happiness is to decide exactly how you define it. Start with the end in mind, begin with a goal, and work back. Engage in the hard discipline of deciding exactly what combination of ingredients causes you to feel the happiest about yourself. You are unique and extraordinary. There's never been and never will be anyone exactly like you. You have a remarkable combination of tastes, values, beliefs, and desires that make your particular definition of happiness different from that of anyone else who has ever lived. Only you can decide what makes you happy. No one can ever dictate happiness to another person. It's a purely subjective or personal decision.

When I think of how different happiness is to each person, I think of a large smorgasbord. Have you ever been to a long buffet line with dozens of different dishes? If you want to see a living example of the differences between human beings, just stand for a short while at the exit end of a buffet line and look at the different combinations of foods that the individuals have put on their plates. You'll never see two exactly the same. The sizes, colors, proportions, and mixtures will be different for each person. This simple exercise proves that neither you nor anyone else can ever decide what will make another person happy. For each person, this choice is his or her primary responsibility in life, and it's both mandatory and unavoidable.

A useful and enjoyable exercise is to write down on a piece of paper the following line: *I would be perfectly happy if . . .* then complete the sentence with as many different answers as you can think of. You might say, *I would be perfectly happy if I had all the money I needed, if I enjoyed perfect health, if I had the love, respect, and esteem of all the people who are important to me, if I were living in the perfect climate,* or *if I were doing the perfect job.* The more detailed your answers are and the more you break them down into clear definitions of exactly what those answers mean, the easier it will be for you to organize your life in such a way that you enjoy far more happiness than the average person.

The silliest thing about happiness is that although everybody wants more of it, very few have ever taken time to decide what it really means to them. This is probably why most people are dissatisfied with their lives. Fortunately, you can free yourself from this tendency by clarifying exactly how each part of your life would be if you were a perfectly happy person already.

Maslow's Hierarchy of Needs

All human action is motivated by a dissatisfaction of some kind. A perfectly satisfied person would have no urge or desire to do or change anything. As a result, the starting point of achieving greater happiness can be an evaluation of some of the needs that you might experience that lead to dissatisfaction.

All human action is motivated by a dissatisfaction of some kind.

Perhaps the most important work in this area was done by the psychologist Abraham Maslow when he postulated his "hierarchy of needs." He said that each person has a series of needs from the lowest to the highest and that each person acts continuously to satisfy these needs.

Maslow explained that until a lower-order need was satisfied, the individual couldn't think or turn their mind to a higher-order need.

He also demonstrated that once a need has been satisfied, it's no longer a motivator. Once you have enough of something you want, you're no longer motivated or driven to get it. Your motivation then changes toward getting something for which you still feel a need.

Maslow's hierarchy originally had five levels of need. In his later research, he suggested that there were two even higher needs. The lowest need, and the first one that must be satisfied, is for survival. Until a person's survival needs are satisfied, until they are no longer concerned about the basics of life—food, clothing, and shelter—they are not concerned about higher needs. Maslow also demonstrated that a person who through accident or circumstance was deprived of a lower need like food would stop trying to fulfill any higher need until the lower need was satisfied once more.

Once a person is assured of survival, he or she becomes concerned with security. The second need up on Maslow's hierarchy is for security of all kinds: physical, emotional, financial.

Once the need for security has been met, the individual turns to the third level: for love and belonging, the need to be accepted by other human beings. People need to interact and associate with other people, to feel themselves to be part of a social group, to be known and cared for by others. This is why solitary confinement is the worst punishment that can be given to the worst criminal in the worst maximum-security institution. Being deprived of the company of others is very painful emotionally.

The fourth level of need discussed by Maslow is the need for self-esteem. This is the need to like and respect yourself and feel you're respected and appreciated by others.

The fifth level is the need for self-actualization. This is defined as the feeling that you are becoming everything you're capable of becoming. Maslow felt that the most advanced and mature members of our society were those who were functioning at the higher levels of need satisfaction. Self-actualized people engage in activities that challenge their abilities and stretch them toward the greater realizations of their full potential.

The two higher needs that Maslow added later were the need for beauty and the need for truth, in that order. Once a person has satisfied their needs for survival, security, belonging, self-esteem, and self-actualization, they would naturally turn to beauty, as in music or art, and truth, as in philosophy or religion. Nonetheless, a person who was functioning at the higher levels of this hierarchy but fell off a boat in the middle of the night would immediately forget about the higher needs and revert instantly to a total concern with survival.

As you mature and become a more fully functioning human being, you find that you're motivated at higher and higher levels of need. The dissatisfactions that deprive you of the happiness you desire are triggered at higher and higher levels. The affluence of present-day Western society has freed more and more people from lower-level needs, enabling them to devote more of their time and thoughts to higher-level needs.

The lower-level needs—survival, security, and belonging—are called *deficiency needs*. Fulfilling them doesn't necessarily make you happy in itself, but being deprived of them can make you very unhappy indeed. The higher-level needs—for self-esteem, self-actualization, beauty, and truth—are called *being needs*. Fulfillment of these needs can lead to feelings of elation, joy, and peak experiences, when you feel wonderful about yourself and life in every respect. These are among the highest states of happiness.

Seven Components of Happiness

In my seminars, I say that everything that you could possibly want in life could be listed under one of seven categories. You tend to measure how well you're doing in life and how happy you are by how much of each of these seven ingredients you have or have not managed to achieve.

The first component of happiness is *peace of mind*. You are happy to the degree to which you can achieve peace of mind. Inner peace is the normal, natural state of humans; deviations from it are unnatural and abnormal. It's important to point this out, because many people think that inner joy is unusual and accidental. Others—very few—realize that this inner experience is the norm and strive to organize their lives so that they have it more often.

The second ingredient of happiness is *health and energy*. Your health, which is largely reflected in your levels of energy, is the minimum requirement for ensuring your survival and well-being. If you gain everything else but lose your health, you are failing in the most important area, but if you maintain high levels of health and energy, no matter what else happens to you on the outside, you're still doing pretty well as a human being.

The third ingredient of happiness is *loving relationships*. You are happy to the degree that other people love and respect you and you love and respect other people. Most of your happiness will come from interactions with the people you care about and who care about you. So developing and preserving loving relationships is a measure of everything you are as a human being.

The fourth ingredient of happiness is *financial freedom*. Most people want a lot of money because it will leave them free to live their lives the way they want, and they feel that this will make them happy. Most material objects and accomplishments are seen as means to this end. But many people make the mistake of confusing means and ends. They become obsessed with getting and spending and lose sight of the reasons for wanting money in the first place.

Financial freedom can be defined as having enough money so that you don't worry about it and can turn your mind and emotions to other, more important subjects. Money is a little bit like a deficiency need: if you have enough of it, you seldom think about it, but if you have too little for any period of time, you think of almost nothing else.

The fifth ingredient of happiness is *worthy goals and ideals*. You experience happiness when you're fully engaged in doing something that is important and meaningful to you. This is why psychologist Viktor Frankl wrote that a need for meaning and purpose is the deepest craving in human nature. Only when you feel that your life stands for something bigger than yourself and that what you're doing is making a difference in the world will you be truly happy.

A need for meaning and purpose is the deepest craving in human nature.

The sixth ingredient of happiness is *self-knowledge and self-understanding*. The ancient Greeks engraved a saying above the temple of Apollo at Delphi: "Know thyself." This advice is more than 2,000 years old, and it's equally true today. You can only be happy when you fully understand why you feel the way you feel and do the things you do. Self-knowledge and self-understanding seem to go hand in hand with inner peace, tranquility, and happiness.

The seventh ingredient of happiness is *self-fulfillment*. It's the feeling you have when you're living your life completely and leaving nothing out. When he withdrew to Walden Pond for two years to think about life, Henry David Thoreau wrote that his primary motivation was to live deliberately and not to come to the end of his years without ever having really lived.

Self-fulfillment is another term for *self-actualization*. This is the need being satisfied by those men and women who have the healthiest personalities and who are the most fully integrated members of our society.

Now ask yourself, in which of these areas might you be suffering a deficiency? In which of these areas are you currently dissatisfied or unhappy? Here's a helpful exercise that you can do on a regular basis. Take a clean sheet of paper and, giving yourself only thirty seconds to reply, ask yourself, *what are my three most important goals in life right now?* Write down the answers quickly, without thought or evaluation.

Then ask yourself the second question: *what are my three biggest worries or problems right now?* Write them down quickly as well.

The answers to these questions will reveal two remarkable things. First, they'll clearly indicate what you need to do or have more of in order to be happy; second, they'll show you what you need to eliminate in order to get rid of unhappiness or dissatisfaction.

Your subconscious mind is remarkable in this way: if you only give yourself thirty seconds to write down the answers to these questions, it will sort through all the millions of bits of data stored in your mental computer and pop the correct answers to the surface of your mind and onto the piece of paper as accurately as if you had taken thirty minutes or even three hours to perform the same exercise. Try it for yourself and see.

The Law of Integrity

In addition to the laws of success and achievement, there are eight specific laws for achieving the happiness you both desire and deserve.

The first is the *law of integrity*. It says that happiness arises as a by-product of choosing to live your life consistently with your highest values and aspirations. Just as Maslow's highest need is truth, your highest need and the foundation of your happiness is living in truth with yourself and with everything and everyone around you.

The slightest deviation from truth, the slightest tendency to compromise with what you know to be right, will detract from your happiness almost immediately. You are designed with an inner guide or conscience that always tells you the right thing to do. You're only happy when you live your life completely consistently with it.

For you to be happy, your goals and your values must be congruent. They must fit into each other like a hand into a glove. Virtually all stress and unhappiness come from trying to do one thing when you believe something else is more important or more correct. For example, most people believe that their relationships, their spouses, children, and families, are more important to them than anything else. But they sometimes become confused and spend an inordinate amount of time achieving material success, ignoring their relationships. The harder they work at their jobs, the more dissatisfied they become, even when they're financially successful, because deep down inside they know that what is truly valuable to them is the people in their lives, not the money.

It's only when you have the courage to insist upon living your life in complete harmony with your highest values that happiness arises. It emerges spontaneously, like sunrise, bringing you the peace and contentment you really want.

The first part of the law of integrity says that when you set goals and ideals that are worthy of you and you strive to achieve them, you'll experience happiness and satisfaction. As Shakespeare wrote in *Hamlet*, "This above all, to thy own self be true, / And it must follow, as the night the day, / Thou canst then not be false to any man."

The second part of the law of integrity says that whenever you choose to live consistently with the very best that is in you, you'll automatically experience happiness and joy. You've probably had an experience where you've decided to walk away from a bad situation, even though it might have been costly either emotionally or financially, but you did it because it was the right thing to do. You acted on a higher principle. You behaved in a manner that was consistent with your highest values. You'll also recall that having done so, you felt wonderful about yourself and your life. You felt tremendous elation and joy. Remarkably, everything turned out all right in the end. The negative consequences that you feared never materialized.

Perhaps the finest example of living in truth—and the most important demonstration of your integrity—is with regard to peace of mind. When you set peace of mind as your highest goal and refuse to stay in any situation that detracts from it, you will enjoying the highest and finest form of happiness.

You are given peace of mind to serve you as an inner barometer. It'll tell you what is right for you and what is wrong. If you listen to your intuition and only do and say what gives you inner peace and harmony, you'll probably never make another mistake.

In her book *The Dynamic Laws of Prosperity*, Catherine Ponder writes that men and women begin to become great only when they take time to listen to their inner voices and organize their lives in such a way that their activities and relationships give them a deep sense of inner peace.

The first step to personal greatness is to sit down quietly and look over your life to determine the areas where you're not experiencing peace of mind and happiness. You'll find that this is a very easy exercise to do, because your mind is continually preoccupied with these problems, just as a person sitting on a tack would be preoccupied with the pain.

Your job is to get off the tack. Your responsibility to yourself is to realize that you can never make someone else happy by being unhappy yourself, just as you can never make someone else healthy by being sick. Do not sacrifice your happiness in an attempt to somehow achieve the happiness of another person. You'll only end up making no one happy, especially yourself.

In the play *Cyrano de Bergerac* by Edmund Rostand, Cyrano, the great individualist, is asked why he is so outspoken and self-assertive. He answers with this beautiful line: "I choose the line of least resistance in this: that I will please at least myself in all things." When you make the decision that for better or worse, you will at least please yourself in all things, only then will you be truly happy. Only then will you be able to help anyone else to be happy as well.

The Law of Emotion

The second law of happiness is the *law of emotion*. It says that human beings are 100 percent emotional in everything they think and feel and decide. I used to think that people were 90 percent emotional and 10 percent logical. However, both research and experience contradict this conclusion. People are totally emotional in everything they do. If a person says he's decided to do the logical thing, it simply means that he has more emotion devoted to that course of action than to another course of action, and he uses the word *logical* to justify his decision.

Human beings are 100 percent emotional in everything they think and feel and decide.

Someone once said that no matter how old you become, you always have the emotions of a teenager. This may or may not be true, but the central impact of your emotions and feelings is a key component in both understanding and achieving your own happiness.

The first part of this law says that you are motivated by two major groups of emotions: those of love or desire and those of fear or loss—the positive emotions and the negative emotions. Sigmund Freud said they are associated with pleasure and pain respectively. You tend to move toward those experiences you associate with pleasure or happiness and you tend to move away from those you associate with pain or unhappiness. This is the essence of the pleasure principle that I mentioned earlier.

The second aspect of this law says that the content of your emotional life is largely determined by the thoughts you dwell upon most of the time. This is such a simple and obvious truth that it's often overlooked. It simply says that if you think happy thoughts, you'll be a happy person. If you think angry thoughts, you'll be an angry person. If you think about the things that people have done to hurt you and the reasons you have to be angry or unhappy, you'll be negative, pessimistic, and eventually depressed. Abraham Lincoln once wrote, "A man is just about as happy as he makes up his mind to be." This is true for you and true for me.

The third part of the law of emotion says that if you deliberately choose to think positive, loving, uplifting thoughts, you can create and maintain your own happiness in spite of what is happening around you. No one can make you feel anything. As Eleanor Roosevelt said, no one can make you feel inferior without your consent. You decide to feel happy and you decide to feel unhappy as a result of the thoughts that you choose to dwell upon most of the time. Therefore the smartest thing to do is to dwell upon thoughts that uplift and enrich your life.

The Basic Law of Happiness

The third law in this session is the *basic law of happiness*, which says the quality of your life is largely determined by how you feel. Because you're 100 percent emotional, how you feel determines your energy level, your personality, your attitude, your performance and output, the clarity of your thinking, the quality of your relationships, and your overall happiness.

Truly successful people enjoy every part of the journey at least as much as, if not more than, they anticipate enjoying the destination. Earl Nightingale once wrote that happiness is the progressive realization of a worthy ideal. It comes from working step by step toward the accomplishment of something that's important to you. It's more a matter of the process than the result, because happiness is experienced in the now rather than at some future date.

The first part of the law of happiness is that how you feel, the quality of your emotional life, is largely determined by how you talk to yourself—your self-talk, your inner dialogue. What you say to yourself on a regular basis largely determines the tone of your emotional life.

The wonderful thing about your self-talk is that it's completely under your own control. One of the best bits of advice I ever read was to immediately override a negative experience by saying something positive and cheerful. Control your own self-talk.

This brings us to the second part of the law of happiness, which says that the way you interpret events to yourself determines your emotional responses to those events. In short, it's not what happens to you but how you react to it that determines how you feel about it. If you interpret an external event as positive or helpful, you'll remain optimistic and cheerful. If you interpret the same event as negative or hurtful, you'll become angry and frustrated, and you'll make yourself unhappy. The choice is always yours.

The third part of this law says that the fastest way to take control of your emotions is to look for the good in any situation. This requires tremendous strength of will, especially when things are going wrong all around you and people are blaming you for their problems. But if you look for the good—even if you just seek out the valuable lesson in each experience—you'll always find it. Furthermore, you can't be looking for the good and be negative or unhappy at the same time. Your subconscious mind can only hold one thought at a time, either positive or negative. If you deliberately choose to hold positive thoughts and dwell upon them, the negative thoughts simply can't get in.

The Law of Substitution

This brings us naturally to the fourth law of happiness, which is the *law of substitution*. It says that you can stay positive by substituting a positive thought for a negative thought. The law of substitution is often called the *crowding out principle*: you can crowd out of your mind any thoughts that aren't helpful to you by choosing to focus your attention on a thought that is more helpful or positive.

Many people are negative simply because they have not deliberately chosen to be positive. They have not systematically planted in their minds the thoughts that are consistent with the emotions they desire to experience. In his book *Learned Optimism*, Dr. Martin Seligman of the University of Pennsylvania says that the great majority of people, who are pessimists, have developed what he calls "learned helplessness." If a person has a series of experiences or makes a series of attempts to do something and is not successful, they unconsciously assume that there's nothing they can do to change things. They perceive themselves to be helpless. From that point on, even when they are given an opportunity of some kind, they will turn it down and give you every conceivable reason why it's not possible for them.

They have tried and failed in the past, so they've now learned to be helpless.

An illustration of this process is the Indian elephant, a huge beast that weighs as much as five tons. Indian elephants are domesticated very early in life and trained to be docile and easily controlled by their owners. The way they do it is simple: When the elephant is a baby, its owner chains it with a large chain to a large stake driven deeply into the ground. The baby elephant struggles against the chain for hour after hour. Finally, the elephant gives up and accepts that when it's chained to a stake, it's helpless; it does no good to struggle; it might just as well stand there until its master comes back and takes off the chain. For the rest of the elephant's life, all its owner has to do is to tie a small rope around the elephant's leg and attach the rope to a small stake in the ground in order to hold the elephant firmly. Even though the rope is small and the stake is shallowly planted, the elephant has learned to be helpless. It no longer struggles or strains against the leash. It may have the strength and the power to knock down houses, but it's completely docile and easily controlled. The elephant's earlier experiences of futility have convinced it that it's powerless whenever it's tied to a stake, no matter how small the stake may be.

Many people are like that elephant: they allow themselves to think continually of the reasons why *not* rather than the reasons *why*. It seems that as soon as you begin to concentrate on how you can achieve a goal rather than on whether or not it's achievable, your mind automatically becomes positive; all your energies become channeled toward achievement and happiness rather than failure and frustration.

The Law of Expression

The fifth law of happiness is the *law of expression*, which states that whatever is expressed is impressed, and whatever is impressed is expressed. Whatever you say, either to yourself or out loud, is impressed into your subconscious mind, and whatever is impressed into your subconscious mind will ultimately be expressed in your thoughts, feelings, conversation, and actions. The more emotion that you use to express any thought or idea, the more deeply it will be impressed into your subconscious mind and the more rapidly it will be reexpressed in your life. Whatever you say with conviction triggers thoughts, ideas, and actions consistent with those words, so be sure to pick your words carefully. When you think of a challenge or a goal and you repeat to yourself the words, *I can do it, I can do it, I can do it,* you trigger all kinds of feelings and actions that propel you toward your goal.

The Law of Reversibility

The sixth law of happiness is the *law of reversibility*. It states that just as your feelings determine your actions, your actions determine your feelings. Even if you don't feel self-confident or happy, if you act as if you have those feelings already, the actions themselves will have a backflow effect and generate emotions consistent with them. When you act in a certain way, the actions trigger thoughts, images, feelings, and attitudes that are consistent with those actions. You can in effect control much of the content of your mental and emotional life simply by moving your body in a way that is consistent with the way you wish to think and feel.

**Just as your feelings determine your actions,
your actions determine your feelings.**

The Law of Visualization

The seventh law of happiness is the *law of visualization*, which states that ideas and images tend to awaken emotions and feelings that correspond to them. When you create clear mental pictures of yourself as happy, positive, and optimistic, they will trigger feelings and actions that actually lead to your being happy, positive, and optimistic.

One helpful exercise is to think of a time in your life when you've been extremely happy and to replay that experience on the screen of your mind as though you are running a movie projector. Put yourself right into the picture and reexperience the feelings that go with it. You can make yourself happy by dwelling upon previous experiences when you've been happy.

The Law of Practice

The eighth law of happiness is the *law of practice*. This law states that whatever you practice and repeat often enough becomes a new habit. Just as you learn to drive a car or type or ride a bicycle, you can train yourself to be a predominantly happy and optimistic person by walking, talking, and acting as though you were happy already.

You begin to become happy when you decide the combination of ingredients in your life that will make you happy and then move toward them. Simultaneously, you need to determine the things that are depriving you of happiness and remove them.

Happiness is an active state or condition that you experience when you are becoming everything that you're capable of becoming and are moving toward the realization of your full potential. It's only when you're doing something that's important to you—something that causes you to strive and stretch towards your limits—that you experience joy and satisfaction. Underlying it all is the law of correspondence, which says that you'll be happy on the outside to the degree to which you are happy on the inside. The truer you are to yourself and the more consistently you live in harmony with your highest values and aspirations, the happier you will be.

The Laws of Happiness

The law of integrity. Happiness arises as a by-product of choosing to live your life consistently with your highest values and aspirations.

The law of emotion. Human beings are 100 percent emotional in everything they think and feel and decide.

The basic law of happiness. The quality of your life is largely determined by how you feel.

The law of substitution. You can stay positive by substituting a positive thought for a negative thought.

The law of expression. Whatever is expressed is impressed, and whatever is impressed is expressed.

The law of reversibility. Just as your feelings determine your actions, your actions determine your feelings.

The law of visualization. Ideas and images tend to awaken emotions and feelings that correspond to them.

The law of practice. Whatever you practice and repeat often enough becomes a new habit.

four

The Laws of Relationships

Your ability to enter into and maintain long-term, intimate, loving relationships with others, and especially with one particular person, tells how fully developed you are. Abraham Maslow, who spent many years studying the happiest and most successful men and women in our society, found that one of their qualities was that they were able to build strong relationships that endured for many years, often a lifetime.

Everything that you've become as a human being is captured in the quality of your interactions with other people. Fully 85 percent of the happiness you enjoy in life will come from your relationships with others.

Unfortunately, this also means that fully 85 percent of your unhappiness and frustration will come from your problems with other people, especially those who are closest to you. It's therefore in your best interest to learn everything you can about forming and enjoying loving relationships.

There are many different kinds of love. Much of what we have learned about love is partially true and partially false, and it's usually somewhat confusing. Sometimes the concept of love is bundled up with romantic love, self-love, love of humankind, or love of animals, nature, beauty, truth, or something else. The scope and quality of the love required to be happy and fulfilled is different for each person.

Just as plants strive upward toward the light of the sun, you as a human being strive continually toward the major sources of love in your life. It's been said that everything we do is either to get love or to compensate for the lack of love. Virtually all personality problems can be traced back to love withheld in early childhood. Many adults spend the last fifty years of life getting over the experiences of the first five years, most of which were associated with inappropriate mixtures of love, punishment, criticism, and negativity.

Everything we do is either to get love or to compensate for the lack of love.

The adult personality is healthy to the degree to which the child received a high quality and quantity of love during the first three to five years of life. If for any reason there was a breakdown of love at this time, the adult will manifest these shortages and deficiencies in their relationships when they grow up.

Sociologist Morris Massey says that as adults, we seek for what we most felt we were deprived of as children. We are subconsciously driven to attempt to fill a void or gap that arose in us in early childhood of which we were almost completely unaware. As adults, in all of our love relationships, we are oriented toward completion and fulfillment of some kind, toward satisfying deep unconscious needs that arose during our formative years.

The brilliant Harvard psychologist and sociologist Pitirim Sorokin studied the phenomenon of love extensively and wrote about it in his book *The Ways and Power of Love*. In this marvelous work, one of the most complete treatments of love ever written, Sorokin describes every form of love and the different qualities that are manifested in it. He talks about the breadth of love: how many people a person can love at one time. He refers to the intensity of love, or how deeply one can feel about another individual. He talks about the duration of love, its specificity, its variability, its stability or enduring power, and several other aspects of the subject. Sorokin makes it clear that love is not a simple thing at all, but because it's so important, it's well worth our while to learn as much about it as we can. Sometimes just a little knowledge of the subject can have a positive effect on our relationships and give us the tools that we need to be happier with others.

Dr. Edmund Opitz, a teacher of mine many years ago, once observed that you can take almost anything to excess except love. He said that love is the one thing in the world that there can never be too much of. I never forgot those words, and over the years I've found that they are as true as anything can be. Perhaps the most wonderful thing about love is that the more you have of it for others, the more of it you have for yourself. The more often that you tell another person that you love him or her, the more love you have for yourself. Love only grows by sharing. The more of it you give away, the more of it you have. Unfortunately, the converse is also true: the less love you give away, the less of it you have for yourself, which goes to explain a lot of unhappiness.

Many parents would agree that one of the great blessings of having children is they teach us more about unselfish, unconditional love than we could ever learn without them. Children in their formative years are like sponges for love. They can absorb love as the desert sand can absorb water. They need love as roses need rain. They can take all the love you have to give them, and more besides. Fortunately, we as human beings are designed not only to seek and receive love but to give love. There's no time that we feel more fully alive and more fully human than when we are pouring out our love to another person. This is why children can enrich their parents out of all proportion to the time, money, and effort they spend in raising them to adulthood.

In this chapter, I want to talk specifically about the love between men and women and how it can be improved and enhanced. There are eleven laws that explain much of what happens between two people, and a knowledge of these laws can help you to be more effective in your most important relationship.

The Law of Commitment

The first law of love and relationships is the *law of commitment*. This law says that the level of commitment is the critical element that determines the long-term health and happiness of a relationship. In study after study, men and women who were found to be the happiest with each other over long periods of time were those who were totally committed to each other and their relationship. They never considered or discussed the possibility of the relationship not working out. It never entered their minds whether this relationship would last. It was an accepted fact, without question or comment, that their relationship was there to stay.

One of the great difficulties in relationships is the *go halfway mentality*. It arises when one or both parties are not willing to make a total, 100 percent commitment to the relationship. One or both of them are hedging their bets and playing it safe. This lack of commitment triggers deep-seated fears of rejection and nonacceptance and leads to a tremendous amount of unhappiness and tension.

One external manifestation of this failure to make a total commitment is the habit of dividing expenses or keeping separate bank accounts. Sometimes people take turns buying things for the house or apartment and keep a careful list of who bought what.

I know a couple who lived together for eleven years but never got around to getting married. He bought the pots and pans. She bought the dishes. He bought the couch. She bought the chairs. He bought the stereo. She bought the television. On every single item there was a little sticker with the initials of the person who had paid for it. At the end of eleven years, they had a quarrel and decided to go their separate ways. They were able to divide up their accumulated possessions in less than two hours, go off in different directions, and never have anything to do with each other again. A lack of commitment that manifested in a continual division of property showed that they were mentally preparing to go their separate ways from very early on.

Another example of this lack of commitment is the prenuptial agreement. Two parties draw up an agreement that specifies how the property will be divided when the relationship collapses. The desire for or insistence upon a prenuptial agreement usually means that one or both parties don't place much faith in the long-term strength of the marriage.

The Law of Value

The second law of love and relationships is the *law of value*. It says that love is a response to value. You always love in another that which you most admire and respect in a human being. This means that love is not blind. You tend to be attracted to a person who you think has qualities that you consider ideal in another.

The first part of the law of value says that when you love and respect a quality or virtue, you tend to love and respect another person who appears to have it. This facet of love can apply to your feelings toward any other human being, male or female, young or old. We all unconsciously tend to give our love and commitment to those people who we feel are most representative of what we value most in others.

Part two of this law says that in a love relationship, you tend to love and be more compatible with another who possesses qualities you admire and which are complementary to your own. Like everyone, you are composed of strengths and weaknesses. Most people have more weaknesses than they have strengths, and since you live with yourself all the time, you're painfully aware of your deficiencies. You also have an innate urge for completion and wholeness, so you tend to seek out a member of the opposite sex who has strengths where you have weaknesses.

Part three of this law says that men and women seek balance and completeness by finding another who appears to be a complement of themselves. When two people are ideal for each other, their personalities balance each other. When blended together, these two people form a single complete person. He is gregarious and outgoing; she is quiet and reserved. He's casual and less concerned with facts and details; she is fastidious and attentive. She is a great implementer, while he is a great planner. He gets upset at silly things, while she remains calm and stable in the midst of chaos. These two people balance each other and combine to make an ideal couple.

The Law of Compatibility

The third law of relationships is the *law of compatibility*, which says people are more compatible when they are similar in beliefs, attitudes, values and ambitions. Compatibility is one of the most important factors in determining the long-term health and happiness of two people in a relationship. Long-term happiness depends upon a high degree of harmony and peace, which is only possible if the essential questions of life are largely resolved and beyond argument.

For example, the number one cause of marital breakdown in America today is disagreements over money. If two people have two different attitudes toward earning, spending, and saving money, it'll lead to continuous clashes. It's only when two people have the same attitudes toward money that it doesn't become a source of argument or disagreement.

The same principle applies to children. It's essential for long-term compatibility that both people possess much the same attitudes toward children, both in having them and bringing them up.

Another area where couples need to be compatible is in the way they spend their leisure time. If he likes the beach and she likes the mountains, or he likes to stay home when she likes to go out, and they can't find ways to compromise, they'll be clashing constantly.

Many people are initially drawn together because of mutual attraction, but it's compatibility with regard to the key values and activities of day-to-day life that will determine the long-term love and strength of the relationship.

Sometimes couples grow apart and become incompatible. This is a major cause of stress, anxiety, unhappiness, and even psychosomatic illness. When incompatibility sets in, the first thing that stops is the laughter. Soon after that, the conversation dwindles away. If they have children, they'll have very little else to talk about except the children; beyond that they really have nothing to say to each other. They have become incompatible.

The best thing to do if you find that you're growing apart is to make every effort to build a new bridge of compatibility. Go for a long drive, take a trip or a long vacation together, and do everything possible to develop new areas of interest and understanding. There are also excellent weekend seminars which couples can attend to rebuild and reaffirm their relationships. There are books that you can read and counseling that you can seek out.

However, if the incompatibility cannot be overcome and you find that you're no longer happy with the other person and you no longer have anything in common, you have to make some hard decisions. Sometimes people hold back from dissolving a marriage because they're overly concerned about what other people might say or think, especially family members. But my experience in dealing with thousands of men and women has brought me to this simple conclusion: no matter what you think other people may say, the truth is that they don't think about you very much at all. It's not that they don't care; it's just that they have so many problems of their own that they can only devote a small portion of their emotional energies to you.

Never stay in an unhappy relationship because of what others might say. Always make your decisions based on what will make you and your partner happy, both in the short term and in the long term. As long as you use your own happiness as a guide for behavior and decisions, you'll be as right as you can be in any situation involving someone else.

**Never stay in an unhappy relationship
because of what others might say.**

The Law of Communication

The fourth law of relationships is the *law of communication*. This law states that the essence of a happy relationship is good communication. Nonetheless, there are differences in the way men and women communicate. In order to communicate well, it's essential that both parties are aware of the differences in communication styles and the differences in both meaning and intention that these styles display.

The first part of this law says that men are direct; women are indirect. Although there are always exceptions to any rules that we attempt to apply to human beings, this one is generally true. Men tend to be direct, straightforward, and to the point. Women, on the other hand, tend to be indirect, roundabout, and subtle. Men tend to resolve differences of opinion by speaking louder and faster, while women attempt to resolve disagreements by finding common ground and approaching the situation with greater sensitivity.

The second part of the law of communication says that you should never assume that you understand what the other is thinking and feeling. If you have any doubt at all, you are probably completely wrong about what's going on. The only way to assure a high quality of communication is to seek to understand the other person before you try to get the other person to understand you. The more you concentrate on understanding, the better will be the quality of your communication and the stronger will be your relationship.

The Law of Attention

The fifth law of relationships is the *law of attention*. This law says that you always pay attention to what you most love and value. You're always attracted to the kind of person that you find most valuable and worthwhile. As your attention goes, so goes your life. Life is merely the study of attention. What attracts your attention in all areas indicates who you are and what is of the greatest interest to you. Your attention and what holds it can often lead you to the right career, the right people, and the right relationship.

The first part of the law of attention says you tend to ignore what you don't value. You do not pay attention to things that you place little value on. If you don't value something at all, you'll hardly even notice it. It won't attract you or keep you interested. Naturally, then, if you ignore or even seem to ignore another person, you send a message to that person that you don't consider him or her to be of value.

Since we often make the mistake of inadvertently ignoring the people we most love, we need to be aware that this attitude on our part, even accidentally, can hurt other people's feelings and lead to problems in relationships.

Part two of the law of attention says that sincere, attentive listening to another is the highest form of love and sensitivity. Patient, uninterrupted listening is one of the highest forms of flattery. It's the way that you tell the other person that you really consider him or her to be important and to be of value to you.

The third part of the law of attention is that listening builds trust, which is the foundation of all lasting relationships. Listening is the essence of excellent communications. It builds the trust that ensures the long-term strength and well-being of the relationship.

Whenever you listen to another person, you tell them in no uncertain terms how much you value them and how important what they are thinking or saying is to you.

The Law of Self-Esteem

The sixth law of love and relationships is the *law of self-esteem*. It's similar to the principle of love in that self-esteem refers to self-love. The law says that everything you do in life is to either increase or protect your self-esteem and sense of personal value and worth. How much you like and value yourself, how much you accept yourself as a worthwhile and important human being, goes to the core of your personality. You are always most attracted to people and situations that build and reinforce your sense of personal value. Simultaneously, you tend to be repelled by people and situations that threaten or harm your self-esteem.

Part one of this law says that you'll tend to be happiest with a person who makes you feel good about yourself. In this sense, love is perfectly selfish. You pick out another person to love because when you're with that person, you feel the best about yourself; you feel happy. In fact, it's common for people to say that when they've met the right person, they have met their best friend; there's nobody they more enjoy being with and talking to and going places with.

The second part of the law of self-esteem says that everything you do to raise the self-esteem of another causes your own self-esteem to go up and makes you like yourself more. One of the wonderful things about doing kindnesses for another person is that everything that you do which makes someone else feel better about themselves causes you to feel better about yourself.

This is an example of the law of correspondence in action. Your outer world tends to reflect your inner world. Your external life tends to be a mirror image of your internal life. Everything you do to make other people feel better about themselves reflects back on you and makes you feel better about yourself.

The third part of the law of self-esteem could be called the *Carnegie corollary* from Dale Carnegie, who first described it in his book *How to Win Friends and Influence People.* He wrote that you can make more friends in a couple of days by becoming genuinely interested in others than you could in a year by trying to get others interested in you. This is one key to truly successful relationships.

The Law of Indirect Effort

The seventh law of love and relationships is the *law of indirect effort.* It says that you tend to get things in relationships indirectly rather than directly. This is true between men and women, parents and children, bosses and employees, and salespeople and customers. The more you approach your relationships indirectly, the more likely you are to be successful. One reason women are rising to the top of many fields today is that they practice this law intuitively in their interactions.

As a result, the more you appreciate and thank others, the more appreciative they will be of you. If you want people to appreciate you, appreciate them first. If you want people to do large things for you, thank them profusely when they do small things for you. When you develop an attitude of gratitude and appear genuinely thankful to everyone for everything they do, you'll be astonished at how warm, helpful, and friendly they'll be in the future.

Similarly, the fastest way to impress another person is to be impressed by him or her. The direct way of impressing another is to try to overwhelm them with stories and examples of what an amazing person you are. The indirect way to impress another is to be impressed by the other person first. The more impressed you are with another, the more impressed they will be with you and your judgment.

A further example of this law is that the surest way to gain the approval and respect of others is to give them your approval and respect in advance. Most men and women who are successful with members of the opposite sex have found that it's very easy to cause another person to be fascinated with you if you simply become fascinated with them in advance. You tend to set up a force field of human magnetism that draws people to you. A man or woman with no extraordinary accomplishments can be very effective in dealing with people in social situations simply by asking questions, listening intently, and being sincerely appreciative of others.

The Law of Reverse Effort

The eighth law is the *law of reverse effort*, which says that the harder you *don't* try in a relationship, the easier it tends to be. You are most effective in your relationships when you rise above the urge to try harder to make the relationship better. The more relaxed and accepting you are of the relationship, the smoother and easier it is for both of you.

**The harder you *don't* try in a relationship,
the easier it tends to be.**

One implication of the law of reverse effort is very important. It says every relationship has its own timing. If you try to hurry it up or slow it down, you merely create resistance and often a crisis. When two people meet, either the timing is right or it's not. At every stage of a relationship, there's a correct time for every major decision, and timing is everything. Research shows that you reach a natural stage in your thinking when you're ready to settle down with one person. Whomever you meet at that point in your life will (assuming compatibility) be the person that you will marry.

At the same time, if you're going through a turbulent period in your inner life, you'll tend to find yourself in a turbulent relationship. You'll tend to attract the kind of person that mirrors your internal psychological state.

The most important part of the concept of timing is that you can't speed things up or slow them down when they involve another person. Often people will meet, go out on a date, and find that they have nothing in common. Five years later, they'll meet again, fall in love, get married, and live happily for the rest of their lives. It's all a matter of timing.

Another comment on the law of reverse effort simply says that sometimes the best thing to do in a difficult situation with another person is the opposite of your natural tendency. If you feel like being angry and impatient, sometimes the best thing to do is to be kind and understanding. If you feel like trying harder, sometimes the best thing to do is to relax and let things unfold naturally. If you feel like speaking up and counterattacking in an argument, sometimes it's best to remain silent and listen patiently until the other person has vented his or her frustrations.

The Law of Control

The eighth law is the *law of control* as it applies to relationships. In this case, it says you are happy in a relationship to the degree to which you feel you have control over what is happening. This is one of the most important single principles of happiness and mental well-being. You need to feel that your primary relationship is largely self-determined and is something that you can change and affect. Whether you feel you have too much or too little control in a relationship, both conditions will lead to problems and unhappiness for both parties.

Part one of the law of control in relationships says that you can increase your sense of control by asserting yourself and taking deliberate action to direct or change the relationship. Sometimes when you feel out of control, it's best to step up, put both your hands on the wheel, and take firm, positive action to change things in such a way that they're more satisfactory to you. Make a decision; get on or get off. Your active decisiveness and your willingness to take action can often resolve a difficulty with another person.

Part two of this law says that you can often assert control in a relationship by walking away. In fact, it's only when you're willing to walk away from a relationship that you're in a position to change it (if change is possible). You must often be willing to end a relationship—to break it up and put it back together on a new basis—if you're going to change or improve it at all. Either asserting yourself or walking away from the relationship can be the solution to your difficulties. Be prepared to try either one in every situation.

The Law of Identification

The ninth law of love and relationships is the *law of identification*. It says that you are dominated by everything and everyone with which you become identified. Everything you take personally and identify with emotionally, everything that you become attached to tends to blur your emotional vision and cause you to be controlled and dominated by it. This is especially true in relationships.

You are dominated by everything and everyone with which you become identified.

The first comment on the law of identification says that you can dominate, direct, and control things only to the degree to which you can disidentify yourself from them. Only to the degree to which you can stand back and be objective about your relationship will you be able to see it clearly and act effectively within it. This is true in virtually every situation in life. That's why they say that a person who acts as his own lawyer has a fool for a client.

The second comment on the law of identification says that attachment and identification cause you to lose perspective and control over your emotions. The more involved you become, the less capable you are of acting in your best interests.

This brings us to the third comment on this law, which is the basis of mental maturity and emotional stability. It says that detachment and disidentification are the keys to peace of mind and happy relationships. They're the keys to self-actualization and personal happiness. You have to be able to put your relationship at arm's length and evaluate it honestly and objectively in order to enjoy it to the fullest.

You'll often have situations where the other person will become very emotional about a particular issue. If you're not careful, you'll also get caught up in it, becoming very emotional yourself. The best thing to do is exert a degree of self-mastery and remain unemotional while the other person is expressing his or her feelings. In this way, you can be of the greatest help to the other person and see things more clearly. By remaining calmer and more detached, you can ensure a greater level of happiness for both of you.

The Law of Forgiveness

The tenth law of love and relationships is one of the most important of all. It is the *law of forgiveness*. It says you are mentally healthy and mature to the degree to which you can freely forgive those you feel have hurt you. This is another way of saying that forgiveness is the highest of all human qualities. It's the key to both spiritual development and peace of mind.

As human beings, we are intensely egotistical and sensitive about ourselves and the way we're treated by others. Whenever we feel that someone has transgressed against us, we become angry and resentful, and we tend to hold on to this anger and resentment far too long. We thereby make ourselves negative, pessimistic, and ineffective in our relationships.

The solution is to freely forgive everyone whom we feel has ever done anything to hurt us in any way, accepting full responsibility for our own contribution to the situation. Whatever it was, you probably got yourself into it through your own conduct and behavior, through your own thinking and decisions. Therefore you are at least partially responsible. The superior person accepts the burden of responsibility and simply lets the negativity go. So forgive others freely, and get on with the rest of your life.

The Law of Reality

The eleventh and final law of love and relationships is the *law of reality*. In its simplest terms, it says, deal with people as they are, not as you want them to be. Don't try to change other people or expect them to change for you.

Part one of this law says that to be happy, you must accept that people are what they are and that they're not likely to change. This is one of the most mature realizations that you can ever reach. Remember the words of comedian Flip Wilson, who would say, "What you see is what you get." Whatever another person is, that's what you get. People are what they are. People take an entire lifetime to become the individuals that you see before you, and they're not likely to change even if they want to. In the absence of some traumatic emotional experience that causes them to question their innermost beliefs and convictions, they'll be pretty much the same indefinitely.

Part two of this law of reality simply says that unconditional acceptance of another is the key to a happy relationship. One of the deepest subconscious cravings that we all have is the need to feel totally accepted. Maslow placed this need for acceptance and belonging as the third basic need in his hierarchy. So instead of criticizing or condemning others, you should just accept them for the remarkable and unique human beings that they are.

Most people don't realize that when they criticize another person or suggest that another person be different in some way, they're actually rejecting that other person and saying that he or she is not good enough for their standards. This triggers deep feelings of fear, inferiority, and insecurity. However, when you unconditionally accept another person and make it clear that no matter what they do or say, you approve of them without question, they will feel terrific about themselves, which will dramatically increase the quality of your relationship with them.

To close this chapter, let me leave you with one of the most important of all principles: you get along with other people to the degree to which you get along with yourself. The law of correspondence in this case is absolute. You can never like or love anyone else more than you like or love yourself. You can never be more accepting or understanding of another person than you are of yourself. So the best way to improve the quality of your relationships is to go to work on yourself. Since you're the only person over whom you have any real control, when you work on yourself rather than trying to change other people, you can really make a difference, and you'll be amazed. You become a better spouse, you'll find that your spouse becomes better. When you become a better parent, you'll be surprised at how much better your children become. The staff becomes better when the manager becomes better, and the customers become better when the salesperson becomes better.

When you work on yourself and concentrate on becoming a better person through study, practice, and reflection, every aspect of your relationships will improve as well. You can make yourself into a superior human being simply by using all of your relationships and interactions with others as opportunities to live out the qualities you want to develop in yourself. You can become any kind of person you want if you are patient enough and if you persist long enough.

The Laws of Relationships

The law of commitment. The level of commitment is the critical element that determines the long-term health and happiness of a relationship.

The law of value. Love is a response to value. You always love in another that which you most admire and respect in a human being.

The law of compatibility. People are more compatible when they are similar in beliefs, attitudes, values, and ambitions.

The law of communication. The essence of a happy relationship is good communication.

The law of attention. You always pay attention to what you most love and value.

The law of self-esteem. Everything you do in life is to either increase or protect your self-esteem and sense of personal value and worth.

The law of indirect effort. You tend to get things in relationships indirectly rather than directly.

The law of reverse effort. The harder you *don't* try in a relationship, the easier it tends to be.

The law of control in relationships. You are happy in a relationship to the degree to which you feel you have control over what is happening.

The law of identification. You are dominated by everything and everyone with which you become identified. Everything you take personally and identify with emotionally, everything that you become attached to, tends to blur your emotional vision and cause you to be controlled and dominated by it.

The law of forgiveness. You are mentally healthy and mature to the degree to which you can freely forgive those you feel have hurt you.

The law of reality. Deal with people as they are, not as you want them to be. Don't try to change other people or expect them to change for you.

five

The Laws of Economics

Some years ago, the Gallup organization completed an extensive survey on 1,500 successful Americans, asking them how they accounted for their great achievements. Most respondents said they felt they had higher than average levels of common sense, which they defined as the ability to have experiences, learn from those experiences, and apply what they had learned to subsequent experiences. As a result, they said they'd become progressively better and eventually leaders in their fields.

These leaders also defined common sense as the ability to cut through the clutter and see the world as it really is. They felt they had a far more honest and objective appraisal of reality than the average person. They didn't delude themselves into wishing and hoping and seeing things that simply weren't there. They didn't ignore the hard facts of life, but rather incorporated these truths into their worldviews and made their decisions and actions based upon them.

This may sound familiar to you, because I have previously called it the *law of reality*. Jack Welch, the legendary former president of

General Electric Corporation, said that it's the most important single principle for success in leadership: in order to succeed in any undertaking, you must be willing to see the world as it is, not as you wish it were. You must conform your life and behaviors to the way the world really is and the way that people really behave, not the way they "should" behave. Abraham Maslow agreed that the ability to be absolutely honest and objective about life and other people is the mark of the fully mature, self-actualizing human being.

To succeed in any undertaking, you must be willing to see the world as it is, not as you wish it were.

In this chapter, I'm going to talk about the laws of economics, but before you roll your eyes and begin thinking that this is a dry and boring subject, I want to point out that economic behavior is simply the study of human psychology and human action. It's the study of how and why individuals behave as they do and how the behaviors of large numbers of these individuals, all motivated the same way, create the economic conditions and possibilities that you see around you every day.

You must understand the laws of economics if you wish to achieve financial success in our competitive economy. The starting point of learning how to make and keep more money is to thoroughly familiarize yourself with the entire subject so that you can anticipate opportunities and avoid economic reversals. An understanding of these laws and principles can enable you to move ahead further and faster than anyone around you. More than anything else, it'll give you a heightened sense of coherence, because you will understand the major events of your world in a way that would escape you if you weren't familiar with these laws.

Because we all have an identical psychological structure, human beings act in certain ways under virtually all circumstances to achieve certain goals. These principles apply to men and women, young and old, educated and uneducated, and they cross all the lines of race, culture, and national origin. They explain many things that otherwise might seem inexplicable. The study of these categories of human action takes us deep into the realms of behavioral and cognitive psychology. They explain the price of apples at your local supermarket as well as budget deficits of billions of dollars. These laws are so clear, powerful, and flexible that you can use them to more accurately interpret your world than you may have believed possible.

The Law of Ambition

The first law of economics can be called the *law of ambition*. In its simplest terms, it says that every act you engage in is an attempt to improve your conditions in some way. Human beings are goal-driven organisms, and they're always driven toward achieving more. Although your goals may change even from minute to minute, from infancy to old age, you are ambitious. You want to improve your life, or some part of your life, in some way. If you're earning a certain amount of money, you want to earn more. If you have a certain level of physical health, you want to be even healthier. If you have one home or apartment, you want a larger one, and if you have a larger one, you want a second one somewhere else. If you have a car, you want a larger car. It's normal, natural, and completely human for everyone to continually strive to get more and better and faster and newer and cheaper everything.

The only limitations on human ambition are those imposed either internally, by the limitations you place on your own mind, or externally, by the limitations imposed upon you by law and society. The twentieth-century Soviet Union spent seventy-four years attempting to create a new type of human being—one who would not be motivated by ambition. That proved to be a total failure. The minute that people saw that it was once more possible to fulfill their ambitions and improve their conditions, there was an outpouring of energy and enthusiasm that swept away the Communist regime so rapidly and abruptly that the whole world stood in wonder, but it was no wonder: it was merely the acting out of individual ambition on a large scale.

This brings us to another version of the ABC theory of human behavior. It says that for you to act, three things are necessary. First, you must be dissatisfied with your existing condition; that's A. Second, you must be aware of a greater satisfaction toward which you can move, and that's C. Third, you must believe that there exists a way, B, to get from where you are to where you want to go.

To restate this, in order for you to act, there must be A, a state of felt dissatisfaction. You must be unhappy with your current situation; you must want to improve things in some way. The C in this ABC formula is your perception of a greater state of satisfaction: there must be something that you want or a condition you can move to that will alleviate your dissatisfaction, like sitting on a tack and jumping off. The B is your perception of something that you can do: a step that you can take that will get you from A to C.

Say you were driving an older car and you saw one of your coworkers driving a brand-new car. This could cause you to be dissatisfied with your car and simultaneously cause you to see that owning a newer car would alleviate this dissatisfaction. The A and the C of the ABC formula now exist. The B could be your conclusion that if you worked a little harder and earned a little more money, you'd be able to afford that newer car. Your heightened level of ambition could drive you toward a more intense effort that would ultimately lead you to satisfy this need.

On the other hand, where you are dissatisfied and see a state of greater satisfaction but you don't see how any action of yours will get you there, you'll refrain from acting at all. For example, you may be driving an old car and you're passed on the road by a Rolls-Royce. You may fantasize about how nice it would be to drive such a lovely car, but you can't even begin to imagine earning the kind of money that would enable you to pay for it. Seeing the Rolls-Royce would not motivate you to act: the A and the C exist, but the B does not.

The difference in levels of ambition is really a difference in levels of desire and belief. If you really believe that you can move from wherever you are to wherever you want to go, you'll be continually compelled to move from A, your state of dissatisfaction, to C, your state of greater satisfaction.

This is the difference between learned helplessness and learned optimism. Most people have pretty much the same abilities and talents as the most successful members in our society, but this majority believes they can do very little that will enable them to fulfill their ambitions. They feel helpless and powerless, so they continue to do what they're doing. Rather than increasing their abilities to accomplish their goals, they decrease their wants and desires so they can be satisfied at a far lower level of accomplishment.

The law of ambition also says that if you're completely contented or if you feel completely helpless, you'll refrain from acting to improve your condition. The only reason that people do not act to continually improve themselves is either that they have reached a state of contentment, feeling that no further improvement is necessary or desirable, or they have reached a state of hopelessness, where they don't think anything they do will make much of a difference. Sometimes these are conscious assumptions—attained by thinking and reasoning—and sometimes they are unconscious conclusions, which you've reached without realizing that they have led you down a mental blind alley.

The Law of Minimum Effort

The second law of economics is *the law of minimum effort*. You always seek to get what you want with the least possible effort. Because you value your time, money, energy and resources, you do everything possible to conserve them. You expend them as carefully as possible to get the things you want. To say that we are economic beings merely means that we are economical in our choices. We don't spend more than we have to in order to satisfy a particular want or need.

The law of minimum effort means that you cannot consciously choose a harder way to accomplish something if an easier way is available to accomplish the same result. You are structured psychologically in such a way that you can't force yourself to select a more difficult path to your goal if you can see an easier path (all other things being equal).

Everyone is the same way, even animals. If you look at a pasture, you'll find that cattle always follow the easiest path to get from one part of the pasture to another. Each subsequent cow follows the same path, wearing a groove that becomes a cow path. You have similar grooves worn in your brain: habitual ways of acting in which you engage automatically and unthinkingly because you've accepted that this is the easiest way to get from one point to another.

The law of minimum effort also says that all human beings are inherently lazy in that they follow the path of least resistance in all things. Laziness, then, is normal, natural, and inherent in all human action. The tendency toward laziness has led to every great advance in science and technology, because every single advance has to be labor-saving in order to be successful. The most affluent countries and companies are those who produce the highest quality of goods and services with the minimum possible effort or expenditure of resources.

The word *lazy* is neither positive nor negative. It's not a value judgment. It's only as you demonstrate this quality that it takes on the value of being either good or bad. If you manifest your laziness by continually seeking faster and more efficient ways to get the things you want, it's a good quality. But if you manifest your laziness by sitting around on a couch watching television, it's a bad quality.

What is the ultimate measure of whether a quality is good or bad? It's simply whether or not the practice of that quality leads to the improvement of the individual's life in the most economical way. If what you do is life enhancing and life enriching, you are using this natural quality of laziness in its highest and best sense.

The Law of Maximization

The third law of economics is the *law of maximization*. It says that you always seek to obtain the highest possible return for your expenditure of time, money, or resources. Again, this is just an obvious explanation of human behavior under almost all circumstances. However, it's extraordinarily important to be aware of this law in order to avoid confusion in interpreting and understanding the behavior of other people.

**You always seek to obtain the highest possible return
for your expenditure of time, money, or resources.**

The first part of the law of maximization says that when given a choice between more and less (all other things being equal), you will always choose more in order to maximize your situation.

The second part of this law says that the desire for more is automatic and instinctive and applies to all human desires and fulfillments. In other words, if you're selling something and one person offers you $5 and another person offers you $6, you'll take the $6 rather than the $5. You'll always choose more rather than less. In order for you to accept a lesser amount, some other higher value must be at work. For example, it often happens that when a company is put up for sale, the owners will accept a lower price from one group of investors because they will promise to protect the jobs and livelihood of the employees while the other group offering a higher price will not.

If all other things are equal, the amount you will demand from the exchange of your time, money, or resources will always be the very most that you can get for the very least that you can give.

This desire for more means that you, like everyone else, are inherently greedy. Again, greed is neither positive nor negative. It's just a fact. Every single person is greedy in that they prefer more to less, although they may be greedy for different things. Even the late Mother Teresa, who was celebrated as a great humanitarian, was greedy in having an intense desire to serve the greatest number of people that she could. Parents are greedy for their children and want the best for them in life. Athletes are greedy in wanting to achieve the most in their areas of competition and to be paid the most for doing it. The only impediment is that most people don't see how they can get from where they are to where they want to go. As soon as a person sees a way of achieving their goals and desires, they take action.

The Law of Time Preference

The fourth law of economics is the *law of time preference*. Because your time is your life and you value your life, you always prefer to have any desire satisfied earlier rather than later. To put it another way, people prefer immediate gratification to delayed gratification, and sometimes they must be rewarded substantially to put off gratification at all.

As a result of this law, when given the choice between a reward today or the identical reward at some future time, in the absence of extenuating circumstances, you'll prefer to take it now rather than later. If someone says to you, "I'll give you $1,000 today, or I'll give you $1,000 in six months," all other things being equal, when would you prefer to have the money?

The answer is obvious. If you have the choice, you'll take it now rather than later. Why? It's worth more now, because you can enjoy what you can buy with that money earlier rather than later.

Because of the law of time preference, you need to be rewarded for delaying gratification. In order to be willing to put off enjoying the reward today, you need to be compensated to a greater degree in the future. For example, interest rates are merely rewards for delaying the expenditure of money to some future period. If you could spend a dollar today or in one year, in order for you to wait for one year, you will want to be rewarded with even greater spending power then. All interest rates are merely rewards for waiting.

Over all of recorded economic history, the average interest rate required for a person to wait is about 3 to 4 percent per year. When interest rates are higher than 3 percent, the extra amount reflects possible inflation, the taxes that might be taken off the interest payment, and the degree of risk involved in getting your money back at all. If any of those three factors is high, the amount of interest that you'll require to delay gratification from the present of the future will be higher still. This is why in some countries with high inflation rates, it's common for borrowers to offer interest rates of 20, 30, and even 40 percent per *month*. These too are merely rewards for delaying gratification and are based on the law of time preference.

The second part of this law simply says that you are inherently impatient in achieving your goals. This impatience is neither good nor bad. Because you value your life, you value your time and the pleasures and gratifications you can enjoy with that time. For this reason, you are always prefer to enjoy these satisfactions now than later. You are naturally impatient: whatever you want, you want it immediately. It takes self-mastery, self-control, and self-discipline to restrain your appetites and delay gratification even though it may be much better and more rewarding to do so in the long run. Children, who lack these developed qualities of constraint, show a high degree of impatience. They want everything immediately.

The Law of Vanity

The fifth law of economics is the *law of vanity*. It says that you are egotistical and self-centered. You place a high value on your appearance, opinions, choices, and relationships and on the way you're treated by others. Each person is ego-centered and vain. Each person is extremely concerned about how they are perceived by others. In fact, much of your personality is determined by the way you think others see you and think about you.

The fact of vanity and the role of the ego in human behavior is not even open to question. The fashion industry, automotive industry, jewelry industry, furniture industry, clothing industry, and many other industries are all built around appealing to the individual's desire to look good to others. Many of the great fortunes have been based on finding a unique and original appeal to vanity with a product or service that can be sold to large numbers of people.

The Law of Ignorance

The sixth law of economics is the *law of ignorance*, which says that every act you engage in is characterized by some uncertainty with regard to the outcome, because you can never know everything there is to know about anything. We are all ignorant to a certain degree, and no one can know everything there is to know about even the smallest subject.

Because we're ignorant, we can't predict with exact certainty what's likely to happen. We don't even know for sure whether we'll drive to and from work on a given day without getting into an accident. Laws of statistics and probability show if we do certain things, like following the traffic laws carefully, wearing seat belts, and driving at a particular distance behind another car, we can improve the odds of arriving safely, but there's still no certainty.

Ignorance is everywhere and all around us. Everyone is ignorant. Most people are incredibly ignorant about an enormous number of subjects, just like you and me. In fact, our areas of knowledge are very small compared to our areas of ignorance. This is why anyone who purports to predict economic trends is really engaging in a form of guesswork. Someone once said that nature is always on the side of the hidden flaw. Murphy's law says that whatever can possibly go wrong will go wrong.

The Law of Expediency

The seventh and perhaps the most important law in understanding economics is what I call the *law of expediency*. It says that people always strive to get the things they want the fastest and easiest way possible, without regard to the secondary consequences of their actions.

People always strive to get the things they want the fastest and easiest way possible

---

The first part of this law says that people are naturally and normally lazy, greedy, ambitious, vain, ignorant, and impatient. This is the way people are in a state of nature, and it's neither good nor bad. It's simply a fact. You are lazy, you are greedy, you are ambitious, you are vain, you are ignorant, and you are impatient, and so is everybody else. We live in an imperfect world because it is full of imperfect human beings.

The law of expediency also means that people strive for security, comfort, leisure, love, respect, and fulfillment in the fastest and easiest ways possible. Each person has a multiplicity of needs and desires, urges and instincts, hopes and dreams, and each person is motivated to achieve satisfaction in these areas in the fastest and easiest possible way, tempered by the fact that they're also vain, ignorant, and impatient.

The law of expediency explains the way the world works. It's often called the path of least resistance. It explains why things go wrong and why people behave the way they do. Everyone in the world is driven in every conceivable way to seek the fastest and easiest way to get the things they want right now without concern for the long-term consequences of their actions.

The Law of Duality

The eighth law of economics is the *law of duality*, which says that there are always two reasons given for doing anything: the reason that sounds good, and the real reason. The reason that people give for doing just about anything is the one that sounds the most socially acceptable and uplifting. The real reason anyone does anything (with few exceptions) is that the individual perceives that this is the fastest and easiest way to get what they want right now.

The first part of the law of duality says that people always give the socially acceptable reason for whatever they do. We call this *rationalization*, which means putting a socially favorable interpretation upon what might be an otherwise socially unacceptable act.

James M. Buchanan of the University of Chicago won the Nobel Prize for his breakthrough work in economics in what he called "public choice theory." He demonstrated that this law of expediency can accurately predict how a politician will behave under any given set of circumstances. The politician's dominant desire is to be elected or reelected. Consequently, you can predict how a politician will vote by studying public opinion polls in that constituency and finding out how many people support a particular policy. The politician, of whatever party, will always vote—irrespective of any principle, philosophical, moral, or otherwise—for the policy that he or she feels will garner the greatest number of votes in the next election. Buchanan received his Nobel Prize because in democratic politics, the law of expediency was extremely accurate in showing how a politician would vote.

The Law of Secondary Consequences

The ninth law of economics is the *law of secondary consequences*, which follows from the law of expediency. Every action will have a direct consequence as well as indirect or secondary consequences. The consideration of secondary consequences is the hallmark of wisdom. The superior thinker is able to look down the road (like a chess player looking down the board), anticipate what might happen as the result of their actions, and take those possible consequences into consideration before acting.

Correspondingly, the law of secondary consequences says that ignorance of secondary consequences is the hallmark of stupidity and the primary cause of failure. Errant assumptions lie at the root of every setback. Action without thinking, along with an unwillingness or inability to consider the secondary consequences of a particular action, seems to precede every failure. The initial reason for acting always seems positive and leads to short-term pleasure or gratification, but the long-term consequences may lead to far greater pain and suffering than could have been imagined.

There's a very simple expression that tends to explain success and failure in adult life: *short-term pain for long-term gain*. If you discipline yourself and sacrifice in the short term through hard work, dedicated application, and saving your money, the long-term rewards can be substantial for you.

The flip side of this equation is *short-term gain for long-term pain*. It says that if you choose to have a good time all the time in the present, the long-term consequences can and will be painful and difficult for you.

This law explains much unhappiness in our society today.

The Law of Unintended Consequences

The tenth law is the *law of unintended consequences*, which says that the ultimate consequences of many actions are far worse than if nothing had been done in the first place. Politics today is a minefield of unintended consequences coming home to roost.

The corollary of the law of unintended consequences is obvious: negative unintended consequences always occur when any action depends for its success on violating the law of expediency. If any law or regulation depends for its success on people overcoming their natural urges to be lazy, greedy, ambitious, selfish, vain, ignorant, and impatient, that law or regulation is destined to fail. You cannot change human nature. You can only organize your society in such a way that men and women eager to improve their lives and following the basic drives of their personalities will act in ways that are productive and constructive for the entire society. This is called free enterprise.

The Law of Choice

The eleventh law of economics is the *law of choice*: every human action is a choice, and the choice is always based on the dominant values of the individual at that moment. You are a choosing organism. You are continually making choices based on what you consider more important and less important. Every act you engage in implies a choice of some kind. You can tell exactly who you are, what you believe, and what's important to you simply by looking at the choices that you make minute by minute, hour by hour, and day by day.

The first part of the law of choice says that your values are always expressed in your actions. As we said before, you always demonstrate what you truly believe and value by your actions. It's not what you say or wish or hope or intend, but only what you do that indicates what you really believe and value.

Your values are always expressed in your actions.

The second part of this law says that you always choose what you most value *at the moment*. When you're walking down the line at a dinner buffet, the items that you put on your plate will exactly reflect the foods that you most value and desire at that particular moment.

The third part of the law of choice says that every action you take or every action you decline to take implies a choice and a statement about your values and beliefs. Now here's an important point: *both actions and inactions have consequences.* Any decision to do something or refrain from doing something has a consequence, and it's based on a value.

For example, if you get up in the morning and you read a book that can help you in some way, you are demonstrating a different set of values than if you get up and watch television and read the newspaper. If you exercise to keep yourself in top condition rather than sitting around talking at lunchtime or after work, you're demonstrating a very different set of values from a person who doesn't exercise. If you read and study or spend time interacting with your family in the evenings rather than watching television or socializing, you are demonstrating a particular set of values. In every case, both what you choose to do and what you choose not to do determine your future.

The Law of the Excluded Alternative

The twelfth law of economics is the *law of the excluded alternative*. It says that whenever you choose to do something, you are simultaneously rejecting or excluding all other choices at that moment. When you decide to marry a particular person, you are simultaneously rejecting the possibility of marrying any other person in the world. When you go out at night, you are excluding all other possibilities at that moment. Every choice implies a rejection of all other choices.

Some people, however, want to have their cake and eat it too. They want to have a little bit of this and a little bit of that. Nevertheless, since you can only choose one thing at a time, every choice is a simultaneous rejection of all other choices. When you purchase a particular item with your limited amount of money, you are at the same time rejecting all other items that are for sale at that moment. You are expressing your highest value with your choice.

Consequently, every choice you make tells what you truly believe and value. Give your choices careful thought, and give your values careful thought as well. Out of them come all the great decisions of life.

The Law of Subjective Value

This brings us to the thirteenth law of economics, one of the great breakthroughs of economic history. The nineteenth-century Austrian economist postulated what has come to be called the *subjective theory of value.* This law says that the value of any good or service is completely personal. It is determined by what a person is willing to pay for it. There are no inherent values in anything. Value is always subjective. People always choose what they feel will make them the happiest or what will most relieve their dissatisfaction at any given moment. No one can choose for another. No one can tell another person whether or not something has a particular value.

When people say that something should be worth a particular amount, they don't realize that the word *should* is meaningless in economics. It merely expresses an opinion, which usually means, "I think that someone else should be made to pay this amount." But in a free society, a mandated or dictated price or wage has very little bearing on the real value of the item. Any attempt to violate an economic law, whether it's the law of expediency or the law of subjective value, always leads to consequences that are far worse in the long run than if the attempt hadn't been made in the first place.

The first part of the law of subjective value says that all prices are educated guesses about how much people will pay to consume the product.

The second part of the law says that all sales at reduced prices are admissions by the vendors that the initial asking price was too high.

The third part of the law of subjective value says only the person being asked to pay is in a position to determine what something is worth. All wages and prices are established arbitrarily, at least initially, but it's only what the customers are willing to pay in the marketplace that determines whether those wages and prices will hold up. If they are too high, people will be laid off or prices will be reduced. The customer in the marketplace will ultimately decide how much will be paid for everything.

The Law of Marginality

The fourteenth law is the *law of marginality*. It's a central law of economics, which says that what the last customer will pay for the last item determines the price of the whole supply. It's not the customer who has the greatest need or the greatest financial resources who determines how an item will be priced in a competitive market; the last customer who can choose between buying that item, buying another item, and buying no item at all will set the final price. Fast-food companies are brilliant at determining what the real price for the marginal customer should be. That's why when they close their doors at night, they've sold virtually everything they've produced that day.

The first part of the law of marginality says that the *market clearing price* is the price at which all customers will satisfy their needs and all sellers will sell all their products and services.

The market clearing price is the essence of both micro- and macroeconomics and is at the core of understanding all economic activity. The market clearing price is the price at which the demand and the supply meet in perfect equality. It's the amount at which all items for sale can be sold, and at which everyone who wants to purchase an item and is willing to pay a particular amount of money can be satisfied.

If the market clearing price is too low, there will still be customers with money who want to buy the product, but there won't be enough of it. If the market clearing price is too high, there will still be items for sale, but customers will be unable or unwilling to purchase them.

The second part of the law of marginality says that the behavior of people on the margin determines all economic activity. For example, it's not the tax rate in general, but the marginal tax rate that determines savings, investment, and productive activity. The amount that a person is charged on each additional dollar of income determines whether or not they will make the additional efforts necessary to earn that income.

The Law of Economic Substitution

The fifteenth law is the *law of economic substitution*, which says that whenever a good or service increases in price, customers seek out substitutes that will yield them the same satisfaction at lower prices. Whenever a good or service or a quantity of labor becomes too expensive, customers begin to seek out lower-price substitutes, and companies emerge in the marketplace to offer them. When American cars became more expensive to own and operate, both Japanese and German car companies saw an opportunity to enter the market with lower prices and lower costs of service.

Many businesses have been built on an individual's recognition that a market opportunity existed to bring out a new product or service that was a satisfactory substitute for something that had been priced out of the marketplace.

In the final analysis, the reality principle rules all. See the world as it is, not as you wish it could be; accept economic laws as facts of life, not problems or difficulties to be resolved. Accept the fact that people act expediently and that within those behaviors lie endless opportunities for success. Accept the fact that people are what they are and that they're not going to change.

Your success will be largely determined by your ability to understand economic behavior as it really is and plan your personal actions for the long term rather than the short term. Successful men and women are long-term thinkers. They have a long time perspective. They look way down the road and they make decisions and take actions today whose fruits will be positive for them and the people around them in the long term. Your ability to internalize and apply these economic principles can have a major impact on everything that happens to you.

The Laws of Economics

The law of ambition. Every act you engage in is an attempt to improve your conditions in some way. Human beings are goal-driven organisms.

The law of minimum effort. You always seek to get what you want with the least possible effort. Because you value your time, money, energy and resources, you do everything possible to conserve them.

The law of maximization. You always seek to obtain the highest possible return for your expenditure of time, money, or resources.

The law of time preference. Because your time is your life and you value your life, you always prefer to have any desire satisfied earlier rather than later. People prefer immediate gratification to delayed gratification.

The law of vanity. You are egotistical and self-centered. You place a high value on your appearance, opinions, choices, and relationships and on the way you're treated by others.

The law of ignorance. Every act you engage in is characterized by some uncertainty with regard to the outcome, because you can never know everything there is to know about anything.

The law of expediency. People always strive to get the things they want the fastest and easiest way possible, without regard to the secondary consequences of their actions.

The law of duality. There are always two reasons given for doing anything: the reason that sounds good, and the real reason.

The law of secondary consequences. Every action will have a direct consequence as well as indirect or secondary consequences.

The law of unintended consequences. The ultimate consequences of many actions are far worse than if nothing had been done in the first place.

The law of choice. Every human action is a choice, and the choice is always based on the dominant values of the individual at that moment. Both actions and decisions *not* to act are choices that have consequences.

The law of the excluded alternative. Whenever you choose to do something, you are simultaneously rejecting or excluding all other choices at that moment.

The law of subjective value. The value of any good or service is completely personal. It is determined by what a person is willing to pay for it.

The law of marginality. What the last customer will pay for the last item determines the price of the whole supply.

The law of economic substitution. Whenever a good or service increases in price, customers seek out substitutes that will yield them the same satisfaction at lower prices.

SIX

The Laws of Negotiating

n his influential book *Frames of Mind: The Theory of Multiple Intelligence*, Howard E. Gardner, a professor of cognitive education at the Harvard Graduate School of Education, explains that there are several different forms of intelligence. Although only mathematical and verbal intelligence are measured during the school years, there are also artistic intelligence, musical intelligence, athletic or physical intelligence, and scientific intelligence. Gardner suggests that everyone has a unique combination of intelligences that makes them capable of performing in a superior fashion—if their particular combination of intelligences is matched to their tasks.

Perhaps the most valued form of intelligence in our society—the one that pays the most, and the one that will make you the happiest—is called social intelligence. In this chapter, I'll discuss social intelligence: the ability to interact, communicate, negotiate, and compromise effectively with other people. Since your interactions with others account for perhaps 85 percent of your success and happiness, it's well worth your while to do everything possible to improve these skills.

The laws of negotiating tie in closely with the laws of economics. Each person places different values on different things at different times, so everyone behaves economically in the sense that they are inclined to negotiate the best deal for themselves. Every financial transaction is based on the law of subjective value, where each party values what the other one has more than they value what they're given in trade. In a free society like ours, commerce and trade only take place when each party believes, based on their individual values, that they'll be better off exchanging with the other than if they didn't.

When you negotiate, you're subject to the economic laws of minimization and maximization: you always want to get the very most for the very least, all things considered. Whenever you're buying, selling, negotiating wages or salaries, or bargaining over the terms and conditions of a purchase or sale, you are negotiating in some way.

In fact, all of life is a negotiation. As an infant, you negotiate for the attention of your parents by crying loudly, and you reward their attention by lying peacefully. Every child knows that love and kisses are a currency that can be traded for food, attention, warmth, toys, and other things, and children learn very early to trade this currency carefully. Since it's all they have to trade, so to speak, they don't spend it freely.

In every relationship, a certain amount of negotiating and bargaining is going back and forth all the time. Even when you drive from one place to another, you are negotiating through traffic, letting other people get in front of you and getting in front of them. When you go to a restaurant, you negotiate to get a table and to get the kind of table where you will feel most comfortable.

It's not really a question of whether you negotiate; the only question is how well do you do it. There are twelve laws of negotiating that will help you to get better deals than you may have ever gotten before.

It's not a question of whether you negotiate; the only question is how well do you do it.

Nierenberg's Law

The first law of negotiating is what I call *Nierenberg's law*, after Gerard Nierenberg, the late expert in negotiation strategy and author of *The Art of Negotiating*. Nierenberg's law says that the aim of a negotiation is to enter into an agreement such that both parties have their needs satisfied and are motivated to fulfill their agreements and to enter into further negotiations with the same party in the future. This is a foundational law of negotiating and needs to be broken down into its constituent parts.

First, the aim of a negotiation is to enter into an agreement. It's not necessarily to win or outsmart the other person.

The second part says that both parties have their needs satisfied. This means that an agreement whereby one or the other party feels they have lost does not fulfill the basic requirement of a successful negotiation.

The law goes on to say that parties are motivated to fulfill their agreements and enter into further negotiations with the same party in the future.

Covey's Law

The second law of negotiating is what I call *Covey's law*, after Stephen R. Covey, who discusses negotiating in his book *7 Habits of Highly Effective People.* This law says in every negotiation, you should aim for a win-win solution, or no deal. In other words, when you enter into a negotiation, you should be clear in advance in your own mind that you will come out with a solution that represents a win for both parties, or you will refuse to make any deal at all.

The first part of Covey's law says that both parties must feel they have won and had their needs satisfied. Part two of the law says in order to reach a win-win agreement, seek for a third alternative that may be different from the initial positions of either party. When you're determined to achieve a win-win solution to a negotiation and you're open, receptive, and flexible in your discussions, you'll often come up with a third alternative that neither party thought of initially but which is superior to what either of you might have come up with on your own.

For example, a husband and wife may want to take a summer vacation, but he's very adamant about going to the mountains and getting a chance to hike, and she's just as adamant about going to the beach and getting a chance to sit in the sun. One or the other could win this negotiation, or they could both stay home—win-lose, lose-win, and lose-lose. Another alternative: they could compromise and spend half their vacation in the mountains and half their vacation at the beach, leaving each of them dissatisfied for half the time. But the best third alternative might be to go to a city like Vancouver, where the mountains meet the sea. With this third alternative, during the day she could go to the beach, and he could go to the mountains. They could be together in the late afternoons, evenings, and early mornings and have a fully satisfying family vacation.

This kind of third alternative solution is almost always available if you're willing to look for it. It simply requires a commitment to win-win negotiating. Deciding that you're only going to agree to a settlement that leads to satisfaction for both parties doesn't mean that you have to accept any arrangement that you consider second-best. With your values and intentions clear, you are in a position to utilize every strategy and tactic available to get the best deal possible for you.

Cohen's Law

The third law of negotiating is what I call *Cohen's law*, which comes from the book *You Can Negotiate Anything* by Herb Cohen, one of America's finest writers and speakers on the subject. His law is simply that everything is negotiable. When you look at life as one long negotiating process, you find that almost every situation contains elements that you can negotiate to improve your level of satisfaction.

Everything is negotiable.

The first part of this law says that established prices are just a best-guess estimate of what the customer will pay. Asking prices are only loosely connected to reality: the cost of manufacturing and marketing a product or service has very little to do with the price that's put on it. Price is arbitrary and, as we've seen, merely reflects someone's opinion of what the market will bear.

The second part of this law says that any written price was written by someone and can be changed by someone. For example, I went into an expensive men's clothing store some years ago and looked at a beautiful $500 cashmere overcoat that had been marked down to $350 and which was prominently displayed on sale. I asked the sales clerk if they would sell that coat for $250. The clerk told me that was impossible: no one ever negotiated prices in this kind of store; what was written on the tag was the price, and it couldn't be changed.

I realized immediately that I was dealing with a person who had no authority, so I wrote down the amount, $250, on the back of my business card and told him to give it to his manager, who was out for lunch. My offer would stay open until 3:00 p.m. that afternoon. I went back to my office. At 2:30 p.m., the telephone rang and the clerk told me that he had gone to his manager, who had agreed to accept $250 for the coat. The clerk was astonished because he had no idea that everything is negotiable.

Dawson's Law

The fourth law of negotiating is what I call *Dawson's law*, which I've named after my friend Roger Dawson. It comes from his audio program *The Secrets of Power Negotiating*. Dawson's law states that you can always get a better deal if you know how. Dawson's first comment on this law is, if you want a better deal, ask for it. The word *ask* is the most powerful word in the entire process of sales and negotiating. Most people are so paralyzed by the fear of rejection that they're afraid to ask for anything out of the ordinary. You'll be astonished at the good deals you can get by simply asking for a lower price if you're buying, and asking for a higher price if you're selling. For example, one of my seminar participants is a real estate salesman who goes out and looks at homes that have come on the market. Whatever the asking price, he offers 50 to 60 percent of that amount, and he offers cash with a very short time limit. He gets turned down dozens of times. But every so often, because of the seller's circumstances, the seller will accept his offer. The salesman can then get a first mortgage for more than he's agreed to pay, which he promptly does, and he either rents the house or resells it at a higher price. His secret is simple: he asks people to sell him their houses at far lower prices than anyone else could ever imagine.

Roger Dawson's second recommendation is that whatever the suggested price, react with disappointment and despair. He suggests that you flinch, no matter what the price or the offer. Appear as if you're in extreme pain and then ask, "Is that the best you can do?" and remain perfectly silent. Often when you ask a person how much an item is and you flinch when they give you the price, they'll lower the price immediately.

Roger Dawson's third comment on this law is, always imply that you can do better somewhere else. Nothing causes a seller's price to drop faster than for you to tell him you can get the same item cheaper from another source.

The Law of Four

The fifth law of negotiating is the *law of four*. It says that in any negotiation there are usually four main issues to be decided upon. Eighty percent of the negotiation will revolve around these four issues.

This law of four and this factor of 80 percent turn out to be valid in almost every case. I've spent two or three days negotiating a forty- to fifty-page agreement full of clauses, subclauses, different details and terms and conditions. At the end I've found that most of the discussion and the most important points of the negotiation revolved around four basic items.

This law also says that of the four main issues in any negotiation, one will be the main issue, and three will be secondary. You can use this law of four extremely powerfully if the other party's order of importance of these issues is different from yours. One party may be more concerned about price, and the other may be more concerned about terms. This can lead to an excellent win-win solution that satisfies the most important needs of each party.

The Law of Timing

The sixth law of negotiating is the *law of timing*. It says that the timing of a negotiation can have a major impact on its outcome. Whenever possible, you must plan strategically and use the timing of the negotiation to your advantage. For example, when buying rental property, the smart negotiator will always arrange to take possession before the beginning of the month. By doing this, the new owner will collect all the cash rents that are due then and will start the period of ownership with money in the bank.

The first part of the law of timing is that the more urgent the need, the less effective the negotiator. If you're in a hurry to close a deal, your ability to negotiate well on your own behalf diminishes dramatically.

The second part of the law of timing says that the person who allows himself to be rushed will get the worst of the bargain. You must be very alert to the fact that this is a well-known truth. Many people will try to get the best of you by running out the clock to the point where you absolutely have to have what you've discussed, and you often have to accept less than you had originally bargained for.

The third part of the law of timing says that the last 20 percent of any discussion will contain the issues and items that account for 80 percent of the importance of the entire discussion. It always seems to be at the very end of a negotiation that the critical elements are resolved and agreed upon.

A final point with regard to timing: whenever possible, you should delay in making an important decision. At the very least, don't allow the other person or persons to rush you into a decision by suggesting that if you don't act now, it'll be too late. Use time as a weapon to strengthen your hand, and improve your ability to negotiate well.

The Law of Terms

The seventh law of negotiating is the *law of terms*, which is a direct outgrowth of the law of timing. It says that the terms of payment can be more important than the price or almost any other factor. For example, I remember the first time I purchased a Mercedes. I told the salesman that there was no way I could afford it. The car was too expensive, and my income simply wouldn't allow it.

I'd purchased cars before and they'd all been financed over a three-year period. The salesman came back immediately and said that because it was a Mercedes and would hold its value, it could be financed over five years. He calculated what the monthly payments would be on a five-year amortization. As soon as I saw the number, I did a complete turnaround and agreed to buy the car, even though it was very expensive. The terms were more important than the price.

The first part of the law of terms says that you can agree to almost any price if you can decide the terms. If you're negotiating and you really want to purchase or sell the item and the price is the sticking point, shift the focus of your discussion to the terms. See if you can't negotiate terms that make the price more acceptable.

Here's a true story that illustrates this strategy. Two older businessman owned land in the Tucson area, and one of them sold his land to a developer for $1 million. A developer friend of mine wanted to purchase the land belonging to the second businessman, which was not as good a piece of land, but the second gentleman also wanted $1 million. As a matter of pride, he didn't feel he could accept less than his friend had received for his land, even though the properties were quite different. In negotiating the terms, however, it turned out that the seller didn't need the proceeds from the land; in fact, they would harm his tax position. He was going to leave the land to his children and grandchildren anyway. So my developer friend agreed to pay $1 million for the land but spread the payments out at a low rate of interest over a period of twenty years. On that basis, the real cost of the land was considerably less, but everyone ended up happy and satisfied. Again, the terms were more important than the price.

The second part of the law of terms says that you should never jump at the first offer. Even if the first offer is everything, you could possibly ask for, don't accept it; act just a little disappointed. Ask for time to think it over. Ponder it carefully. Realize that no matter how good the first offer is, it just means that you can get an even better deal if you're patient.

Never jump at the first offer.

The Law of Preparation

The eighth law of negotiating is perhaps the most important of all. It's the *law of preparation*. It states that fully 80 percent of your success in any negotiation will be determined by how well you prepare in advance. Just as action without planning is the cause of every failure, negotiating without preparation is the cause of most poor deals. The best negotiators take the time to prepare the most thoroughly and think through the situation completely before the negotiation begins.

The first part of this law could be called *Geneen's rule* from Harold Geneen, the president of ITT during the period when it grew into an international conglomerate composed of more than 150 companies. He was adamant about this rule: *get the facts.*

You must take the time to get the facts prior to any negotiating situation. Avoid the tendency to accept superficial answers or incomplete numbers. Don't leap to conclusions. Ask questions; listen carefully. Do your research and take notes. This can make an extraordinary difference to the outcome.

The second part of the law of preparation says, *do your homework.* One small detail may be all you need to succeed in a negotiation. A book by the famous trial lawyer Louis Nizer entitled *My Life in Court* explained how over a career spanning more than 100 major trials, he was able to win life-and-death cases for his clients because of his exhaustive preparation. Sometimes one small fact that he'd been able to uncover in many hours of research made all the difference.

The third part of the law of preparation says, *check your assumptions.* Always ask, what are my assumptions, and what if I was wrong? Incorrect assumptions lie at the root of many failures. When in doubt, ask questions of anyone who can help you. As a simple example, when going into a negotiation, almost everyone assumes that the other party wants to make a deal in the first place. This may not be the case at all. You need to test this assumption. Sometimes the other party is only negotiating with you to increase his leverage with someone else, so never assume.

Here's another example. Almost everyone in sales is on a monthly quota. In the first half to three quarters of the month, most salespeople are not too worried about reaching their quotas. However, in the last week of the month the pressure is on. You can almost always get a better deal in purchasing any large item if you do your tire kicking early in the month and you do your negotiating in the last couple of days of the month. Knowing that one small detail can give you an edge that can save or gain you hundreds, even thousands, of dollars over the course of your negotiating lifetime.

The Law of Reversal

The ninth law of negotiating is the *law of reversal*. This law says that putting yourself in the situation of the other person first enables you to prepare and negotiate more effectively. Before any negotiation of consequence, use the lawyer's method of preparation in reverse. Student lawyers are often given a case to either prosecute or defend as an exercise. They're then taught to prepare the other lawyer's case before they begin preparing their own. They sit down and look at all the information and evidence, and they imagine that they are on the other side. They prepare that side thoroughly with a full intention of winning. Only when they feel they've covered all the bases from the other point of view do they begin to prepare their side of the issue.

A good exercise is to sit down with a pad of paper and write down everything that you think may be of concern to the person with whom you're going to negotiate. Writing things down clarifies them in such a way that you can often see possibilities that you might otherwise have overlooked. When you've identified the major things that you think the other party will want, you can decide what you'll offer in exchange, where you're strong, where you're weak, and where there are possible areas for compromise. This type of preparation by reversal is the hallmark of the superior negotiator.

Another helpful tactic is to ask the other person at the beginning of the negotiation, why do you feel we are here, and what would you ideally like to accomplish in this discussion? This simple question will demonstrate to the other party that you're reasonable, open, and interested in achieving a mutually satisfactory result. The other person will usually be quite willing to answer this question, and you'll be amazed at the results.

The Law of Power

This brings us now to the inner game and to the tenth law of negotiating: *the law of power*. This law says that the person with the greater power, real or imagined, will get the better deal in any negotiation.

The first part of the law of power says that no one will negotiate with you unless they feel that you have the power to help them or hurt them in some way.

The second part of this law says that power is a matter of perception; it's in the eye of the beholder. Negotiator Herb Cohen says that the three most important keys to negotiating are power, preparation, and timing, and of these three, power is often the most important and the most influential.

Ten Types of Power

There are ten different types of power that you can develop and use either individually or collectively to influence the other party in any negotiation. The more important the issue, the more time you should take to consider how you can utilize one or more of these elements to strengthen your position.

The first is the *power of indifference.* The party who appears to be the most indifferent to whether or not the negotiation succeeds often has power over the other person—if that person has a greater stake in the outcome. Whenever possible, you should appear slightly detached and indifferent, as though you don't really care one way or the other.

The second form is the *power of scarcity.* Whenever you can suggest or imply that the item you're selling is in scarce supply and that there are others who want it, you can influence the negotiation in your favor.

The third form of power is that of *authority.* When you have an impressive title or you look as though you have the authority to make big decisions, this image alone often intimidates the other person and enables you to get a better deal.

The fourth form of power is that of *courage.* You build perception of this power by being willing to take risks, to speak out clearly and forcefully, and to either put yourself on the line for this deal or walk away from it.

The fifth type of power is that of *commitment.* When you appear totally committed to success in an enterprise, you radiate an aura of power that often causes people to cooperate.

Sixth is the power of *expertise,* which comes from your making it obvious that you're extremely well-informed on the subject under negotiation. A person who is perceived as an expert in any situation has power over those who don't feel as knowledgeable.

The seventh form of power is *knowledge of the needs of the other.* The more time you take to find out exactly the situation of the other person, the more power you have in the negotiation.

Eighth is the power of *empathy*. Human beings are intensely emotional in everything they do and say. When they feel the person they're negotiating with has a high level of empathy with them and their situation, they're much more likely to agree to beneficial terms.

By the way, every study of top negotiators shows that they are highly empathetic, low-key, solution-oriented, and pleasant individuals to do business with. The picture of the tough-talking negotiator is largely fictitious. Good negotiators are very nice people, and they make it clear from the beginning that they really care about reaching an agreement that everyone can live with.

The ninth form of power in negotiating is that of *rewarding or punishing*. When the other party perceives that you can help them get something they want or withhold something from them, they're often far more cooperative.

Tenth is the power of *investment*, either of time or money or both. When you make it clear that you've invested a lot in the issue under negotiation, it gives you a power that you wouldn't have had if you had spent less time and effort. It also gives you power to know that the other person has invested a lot in the negotiation.

For example, when I purchased my current house, I sat down with the owner and told him that my wife and I had looked at more than 150 houses and this was the first one that we decided to make an offer on. Even though the seller had only had the house on the market for a few weeks, he recognized immediately that we were serious. He negotiated with us in a serious way, leading ultimately to a satisfactory sale for him and a satisfactory purchase for us. If we had told him that this was one of the first houses we looked at, his attitude might have been completely different.

In any case, your choice in negotiating is either to be influenced by or to influence the other party. The more of these elements of power that you can bring to bear in a negotiation, the more persuasive and effective you will be.

The Law of Desire

The eleventh law of negotiating is the law of desire: the person who most wants the negotiation to succeed has the *least* bargaining power.

The first part of this law says that no matter how badly you want it, you should appear neutral or only mildly interested. The more important it is to you, the more important it is for you to appear unemotional, unaffected, and unreadable. Don't smile or appear really interested in any way.

The second part of this law says that the more you can make the other party want the item under negotiation, the better deal you can get. This of course, is the essence of successful selling. Desire is a critical element. Chinese jade dealers were famous for showing one item of jade jewelry at a time to a prospective customer. The Chinese, by long custom, would keep their faces completely unemotional and unreadable. However, when the jade dealer revealed a piece that the customer really liked, the pupils of the customer's eyes would dilate widely. The jade dealer would be watching carefully for this: when he saw the pupils dilate, he knew which item the customer wanted most and which item to negotiate on the hardest.

The Law of Reciprocity

The twelfth law of negotiating is the *law of reciprocity*, which states that you are strongly motivated to pay people back for anything they do for you. This law of reciprocity is one of the most powerful of all subconscious drives. There is within each person an intense desire to be even with others. If a person does something nice for us, we feel that we're under an obligation, and we seek every opportunity to do something nice back so that we can even the score.

You are strongly motivated to pay people back for anything they do for you.

The law of reciprocity is most obvious in negotiating when the issue of concessions comes up. The first part of this law says that the first party to make a concession will be the one who wants the deal the most. You must therefore avoid being the first one to make a concession, even a small one. Instead, remain silent. The first party to make a concession will tend to make additional concessions. most purchasers or sellers are aware of this fact, so be careful.

The second part of the law of reciprocity says that every concession you make in a negotiation should be matched by an equal or greater concession by the other party. If the other party asks for a concession, you may grant it, but never without asking for something else in return. If you don't request a reciprocal concession, the one that you grant will be considered to have little value, and it won't help you as the negotiation proceeds. Even if the concession is of no importance to you, always attach it to a concession by the other side.

The third part of the law of reciprocity says to make small concessions on small issues so that you can ask for reciprocity or concessions on large issues. One of the best negotiating strategies is to be willing to give in order to get. When you make every effort to appear reasonable by conceding on issues that are unimportant to you, you put yourself in an excellent position to request an equal or greater concession later.

The Walkaway Law

The thirteenth law, the *walkaway law of negotiating*, states that you never know the final price and terms until you get up and walk away. You may negotiate back and forth for a long time and haggle in detail over prices and terms, but you never really know the best deal you can get until you make it clear that you are prepared to walk out of the negotiation completely.

The first part of the walkaway law says that the power is on the side of the person who can walk out without flinching. When you do walk out, always be pleasant, low-key, and polite. Leave the door open so that you can enter back into the negotiation with no loss of face.

The second part of this law says that walking out of a negotiation is just another way of negotiating. Some of the best negotiators, both nationally and internationally, are extremely adept at getting up and walking out. They will even leave the room, leave the building, the city, and even the country if necessary to strengthen their hand and increase their perceived power.

It's quite common when teams are negotiating for two or three key players on one team to get up angrily, storm out of the room, and vow never to come back. However, they will leave someone behind who will seek for some way to make peace with his partners and bring them back into the discussion. Sometimes this is called *good guy, bad guy*. Of the two types of negotiators, one will be hard and demanding, while the other will be friendly and accommodating. It's all part of the game. You need to be aware of it in case anyone ever tries to use it on you.

The Law of Finality

The fourteenth law of negotiating, the *law of finality*, states that no negotiation is ever final just because you've reached an agreement and it's signed, sealed, and delivered.

Remember the first law of negotiating, which says that the purpose of a negotiation is to enter into an agreement such that both parties have their needs satisfied and are motivated to fulfill their commitments and enter into subsequent negotiations with the same party. It often happens that once a negotiation is complete, one or both parties think of something or become aware of an issue that hasn't been satisfactorily resolved; maybe circumstances have changed between the signing of the agreement and its implementation. In any case, one party is no longer happy with the result of the negotiation and feels they have lost.

The first part of the law of finality says that if you're not happy with the existing agreement, ask to reopen the negotiation. Remember, most people are quite reasonable: they want you to be happy with the terms agreed upon, especially if the terms are to be carried out over a long period of time. If you find that you're not happy with a particular term or condition, before you go back to the other party, think of some reason it would be beneficial to them to make these changes. Don't be afraid to point out that you're not happy with the agreement and that you'd like to change it to be fairer and more equitable.

The second part of the law of finality says, use zero base thinking on a regular basis by asking yourself, if you had it to do over, would you agree to the same terms?

Remember that negotiating is a normal and natural part of life and you owe it to yourself to become very good at it. As in anything else, the key to excellence is to practice at every opportunity. Make it a game: ask for better prices, better terms, better conditions, better interest rates, and better everything. You can save yourself the equivalent of months and even years of hard work by learning how to become an excellent negotiator on your own behalf—and you can if you think you can.

The Laws of Negotiating

Nierenberg's law. The aim of a negotiation is to enter into an agreement such that both parties have their needs satisfied and are motivated to fulfill their agreements and to enter into further negotiations with the same party in the future.

Covey's law. In every negotiation, you should aim for a win-win solution, or no deal.

Cohen's law. Everything is negotiable. Almost every situation contains elements that you can negotiate in order to improve your level of satisfaction.

Dawson's law. You can always get a better deal if you know how.

The law of four. In any negotiation, there are usually four main issues to be decided upon.

The law of timing. The timing of a negotiation can have a major impact on its outcome.

The law of terms. The terms of payment can be more important than the price or almost any other factor.

The law of preparation. Fully 80 percent of your success in any negotiation will be determined by how well you prepare in advance.

The law of reversal. Putting yourself in the situation of the other person enables you to prepare and negotiate more effectively.

The law of power. The person with the greater power, real or imagined, will get the better deal in any negotiation.

The law of desire. The person who most wants the negotiation to succeed has the *least* bargaining power.

The law of reciprocity. You are strongly motivated to pay people back for anything they do for you.

The walkaway law of negotiating. You never know the final price and terms until you get up and walk away.

seven

The Laws of Money

One major ingredient of happiness—and one of the most important needs that you must satisfy—is the need to obtain enough money so that you don't need to worry about it. I've already discussed the law of cause and effect and its sublaw, the law of belief. There's perhaps no other area where these laws are more in evidence than in the acquiring and keeping of money. Hundreds of thousands of men and women have started with nothing or even deeply in debt and achieved financial independence. Their attitudes and behaviors have been studied extensively, so we now know the causes of financial freedom better than ever before. Your most cherished beliefs on this subject will primarily determine how much you get and how much you keep over the course of your working lifetime.

One of the deepest needs of human nature is to feel financially secure and safe. You can only free yourself from the fear of poverty and failure by achieving a certain financial estate and building a fortress around it so that you're safe and impregnable. Achieving financial independence must be one of your primary duties and responsibilities, because no one else will do it for you. As I've said, money is a deficiency need: when you have enough, you don't think much about it, but when you have too little, you think of nothing else. Money problems are a primary reason for marital breakdown, business collapse, the ruination of friendships, and psychosomatic illnesses of all kinds.

The reality principle, or the law of reality, holds true with regard to money: you must deal with life as it is, not as you wish it were. Many people live in a world of self-delusion, where they wish and hope and pray about certain goals which they know deep in their hearts will never materialize.

Perhaps the most common difficulty that people have in obtaining financial independence is a deep-seated belief that somehow money is wrong and people who have a lot of it are inherently evil. This belief isn't based on any factual foundation, but goes back to early childhood conditioning: the growing child is often convinced of this idea because of adults' desires to rationalize away their own financial failures.

When my wife and I got married, her entire family attended the wedding, as did my employer, a man worth more than $500 million. All their lives, the members of my wife's family had been led to believe that poverty was a virtue and by extension that financial success was somehow unclean or evil.

They were astonished to find that my employer, the richest man they'd ever met, was devoutly religious. He was a solid family man, very low-keyed, polite, courteous, and charming. It took them months, even years, to readjust their thinking, because they'd been led to believe that anyone with that kind of money must be bad in some way.

The fact is that money is good, and it's largely attracted to good people. Money buys freedom. It gives you choices and enables you to live your life the way you want. It opens doors for you that would have been closed in its absence.

Money is good, and it's largely attracted to good people.

Just like anything, an obsession with money can be hurtful. The Bible says the love of money is the root of all evil (1 Timothy 6:10). It doesn't say that *money* is the root of all evil: it says that the *love* of money is the root of all evil. It's the preoccupation with money to the exclusion of the really important things in life that is the problem, not the money itself. Money itself is neither good nor bad. It's only the way it's acquired and the uses to which it's put that imposes any value on it at all.

Money tends to flow toward those people who can use it in the most productive way to create goods, services, employment, and activities that benefit many others. At the same time, money flows away from those who use it poorly or nonproductively. Money is very much like a lover: it must be courted, coaxed, flattered, and treated with care and attention. It gravitates toward people who respect and value it and are capable of doing worthwhile things with it. It flows through the fingers of people who don't understand it or take proper care of it.

Some people say they're not very good with money. Usually that's merely a rationalization for the fact that they are not very successful with money when they simply haven't learned how to acquire or hold on to it. But being good with money is a skill that anyone can learn through practice.

The starting point of accumulating money is to begin to believe that you have an unlimited capacity to obtain all the money you'll ever need. Look upon yourself as a series of financial opportunities just waiting for a place to happen.

There are thirteen laws of money that you can apply to acquire and keep more of it.

The Law of Abundance

The first is *the law of abundance*. This law states that there's an ample supply of money for everyone who really wants it and who obeys the laws of cause and effect as they apply to money. There's plenty of money around and available to you. There's no real shortage. You can have virtually all you want and need.

The first part of the law of abundance says that people are rich because they decide to be rich. You can also say that they're rich because they believe they have the capacity to become rich. In so believing, they take the necessary actions that turn their beliefs into realities.

The second part of this law is that people are poor because they haven't yet decided to be rich. In his book *Instant Millionaire*, Mark Fisher asks the question, why aren't you rich already? How you answer will reveal a lot about you. Your answers will expose your self-limiting beliefs, your doubts, fears, excuses, rationalizations, and justifications.

Why aren't you rich yet? Write down your answers on paper. Whatever they are, it's up to you to remove the obstacles between you and the amount of money you wish to acquire.

The Law of Exchange

The second law of money is the *law of exchange*. It states that money is the medium through which people exchange their production of goods and services for the goods and services of others. Before there was money, there was barter, whereby people exchanged goods and services directly for other goods and services. As civilization grew and barter became too clumsy, people found that they could exchange their goods and services, for a medium like coins, which they could then exchange for the goods and services of others. Today we exchange our work for money, which we use to purchase the results of the work of other people.

The first part of the law of exchange says money is a measure of the value that people place on goods and services. In the laws of economics, I described the law of subjective value: the fact that it's only what someone will pay that determines the value of a given item. Every item for sale is priced based on what someone will exchange for it.

The second part of this law says that your labor is considered a cost by everyone else. We tend to look upon the sweat of our brow as something special because it's so intensely personal. However, we can't place a value on our own labor: it's only what other people are willing to pay for our labor in a competitive marketplace determines what we are worth. Earl Nightingale once said that you'll always be paid in direct proportion to the work you do, how well you do it, and the difficulty of replacing you. The quantity and quality of your contribution in comparison with those of others, and the value that people place on those contributions, will determine exactly how much you're paid.

The law of exchange also says that money is an effect, not a cause. Your work, or your contribution to the value of a product or service, is the cause, and the wage, salary, or earnings that come out is the effect. If you wish to increase the effect, you have to increase the cause.

Furthermore, the law of exchange says that to increase the amount of money you're getting, you must increase the value of the work that you're putting in. To earn more money, you must increase your knowledge or skill, improve your work habits, work longer and harder hours, work more creatively, or do something else that enables you to better leverage your talents. Sometimes you have to do all of these together. The highest-paid people in our society are those who are using more of these factors in coordination so as to add dramatic value to their work.

The Law of Capital

The third law of money is the *law of capital*, which states that your most valuable asset in terms of cash flow is your physical and mental capital, your earning ability. You may not even be aware of this fact, but by utilizing your earning ability to its fullest, you can pump thousands of dollars per year into your life and generate sufficient money to pay for all the things that you want and more besides. The amount of money that you are paid is a direct measure of the extent to which you've developed your earning ability so far.

The first part of the law of capital says that your most precious resource is your time. Your time is really all you have to sell. How much time you put in and how much of yourself you put into that time largely determines your earning ability. Poor time management is one of the major reasons for underachievement and failure.

The second part of the law of capital says that time and money can be either spent or invested. To a certain degree, your time and your money are interchangeable. You can spend your money to save time, or you can spend your time to save money. You can spend your time or money, in which case they're gone forever. Or if you choose, you can invest your time or your money or both and get a return on your investment.

One of the smartest things that you can do is to invest 3 percent of your income, or more, every month and one hour of your time every day into increasing your earning ability and building your human capital. This commitment to personal and professional development will pay off in greater measure than you can believe. Your return on the investment of your time and money into yourself can be extraordinary. The head of training for Motorola at one point estimated that his company was getting $30 back for every dollar they invest in training. He said that it was the highest payoff that the company could receive. They increased their expenditures to 4.8 percent of gross sales to invest in training. Therefore one of the best investments of your time and money is into increasing your earning ability.

The Law of Time Perspective

The fourth law of money is the *law of time perspective*. This comes from pioneering work in sociology and success conducted by Edward Banfield of Harvard University in the late fifties and early sixties. After studying the factors that were thought to contribute to financial success, he concluded that one factor seemed to take precedence over all the others, which he called *time perspective*: the most successful people are those who take the longest time period into consideration when making their day-to-day decisions.

The most successful people are those who take the longest time period into consideration when making their decisions.

Banfield found that the higher up you go in any society, the longer the time perspective of the people at that level. An obvious example is the man or woman who spends ten or twelve years studying and interning to become a doctor. This person takes an extraordinarily long time to lay down the foundation for a lifetime career.

As you go down each rung of the socioeconomic ladder, individuals have increasingly short time perspectives. At the bottom of the ladder, the hopeless alcoholic or drug addict has a time perspective that is less than one hour. You begin to elevate yourself socially and financially the day you begin thinking about what you're doing in terms of the possible long-term consequences of your actions and inaction.

The first part of the law of time perspective says that delayed gratification is the key to financial success. Your ability to resist the law of expediency, which urges you to satisfy your desires the fastest and easiest way possible, is the starting point of developing a long time perspective. This attitude is essential to financial achievement.

The second part of this law says that self-discipline is the most important quality for long-term success. Your ability to discipline yourself is probably the most important single quality that you can develop in your movement toward greater success and accomplishment.

The third part of this law says that sacrifice in the short term is the price you pay for security in the long term. The key word here is *sacrifice*. Parents who work hard and save their money so that their children will be able to get an excellent education are practicing long time perspective. They're making decisions that can affect their children and future generations.

The Law of Saving

The fifth law of money is the *law of saving*: financial freedom comes to individuals who save 10 percent or more of their income throughout their lifetimes. One of the smartest things that you can ever do is to develop the habit of saving part of your salary from the time you take your first job. Individuals, families, and even societies are stable and successful to the degree to which they have high savings rates. Savings today guarantees the security and possibilities of tomorrow.

The first part of the law of saving comes from the famous book entitled *The Richest Man in Babylon* by George Clason. In it, he recommends that you save 10 percent of your income in a fund for long-term financial accumulation. His rule is pay yourself first: however much you earn, take 10 percent off the top and pay it to yourself in the form of a long-term savings or investment account before you pay your regular operating expenses. Remarkably, when you pay yourself first and force yourself to live on the other 90 percent, it soon becomes fairly easy. Many people go from paying themselves first with 10 percent of their income to eventually saving 15 and 20 percent and even more, and their financial lives changed dramatically as a result.

The second part of the law of savings says, take advantage of tax-deferred savings and investment plans. Because of high tax rates, money that is saved or invested without being taxed accumulates at a rate of 30 to 40 percent faster than money that's subject to taxation. In his book *Wealth without Risk*, Charles Givens lays out a variety of strategies for saving money on your day-to-day expenses and putting it carefully away so that it accumulates over time to ultimately bring you the financial security that you desire. He strongly recommends tax-deferred savings.

The third part of this law says that once you start a savings program, never use the money for anything but financial accumulation. It's sad but true that if you save for a rainy day, the one thing you can be sure of is that it's going to start raining very soon. If you save with the intention of spending the money as soon as you need it, you're going to need it sooner than you realize. Your philosophy of savings should be that once you put the money away, you never spend it on anything. If you want to save for a rainy day or a car or house, you set up separate savings accounts for them, but once you've begun your wealth accumulation account, you discipline yourself never touch it and not for any reason.

The Law of Conservation

Sixth is the *law of conservation*, which says that it's not how much you make but how much you keep that will determine your financial future. Many people make a lot of money in the course of their working lifetimes. Sometimes during boom periods people greatly exceed their expectations and make more money than they ever thought possible. Unfortunately, they develop the walk on water syndrome and begin to believe that it's because of their remarkable skills and abilities that they're doing so well. In many cases, it's just because the economy or that particular field is booming. These people often assume that because they're making a lot of money, they have the ability to make it indefinitely and go on to spend everything they earn.

The true measure of how well you're doing is how much you keep out of the amount that you earn. Successful people are fastidious about putting away chunks of money and paying down debt during the prosperous times so that they have a solid financial foundation that isn't threatened when the economy or business turns downward.

Parkinson's Law

The seventh law of money is *Parkinson's law*. It is one of the best-known and most important laws of money and wealth accumulation. Put forth by the British author C. Northcote Parkinson many years ago, it says simply that expenses always rise to meet income. No matter how much people make, they tend to spend the whole amount and a little bit more besides. Expenditures always seem to rise to meet income.

The first part of Parkinson's law is extremely important: financial security comes from *violating* Parkinson's law. Only to the degree to which you resist the powerful urge to spend everything you make can you begin to build your financial fortress and move ahead of the crowd.

The second part of Parkinson's law is that if you allow your expenses to increase at a slower rate than your income and you save or invest the difference, you'll become financially independent in your working lifetime. I call it the *wedge*: if you can drive a wedge between your increasing earnings over time and the increasing cost of your lifestyle and save or invest the difference, you can continue to improve your lifestyle as you make more money. By violating Parkinson's law, you'll end up financially well off.

The Law of Three

The eighth law is the *law of three*, which says there are three legs to the stool of financial freedom: savings, insurance, and investment. One of your jobs is to build a financial fortress for yourself within which you can be safe from the insecurities experienced by most people in old age. Throughout your working lifetime, you need to maintain a certain amount in each of these three categories.

The first part of the law of three says that your savings should be liquid and sufficient for two to six months of normal expenses. Your first job financially is to save enough money so that if you lost your source of income for up to six months, you'd have enough put aside to carry you over. The very act of saving this amount of money and putting it into a high-yielding savings or money market account will give you a tremendous sense of confidence and inner peace.

A young woman who attended one of my seminars wrote to me after a year and told me an interesting story. She said that she had never considered the fact that she was completely responsible for her own financial well-being. From that moment forward, however, she began saving some of her income from every paycheck rather than spending it all as she earned it, as she had done in the past. She became so good at saving that within a year, she had almost two months of income put aside in the bank.

About that time, she began to have difficulties with her boss and eventually walked out of her job. She said that having the money in the bank made it possible for her to quit doing something she no longer enjoyed and allowed her to take her time finding a better job, at which she was paid substantially more. She wrote that if she hadn't started saving, she would have been trapped in her job. She would have been unable to leave and would have lost her self-respect and her self-esteem.

The second part of the law of three says that you should carry sufficient life and health insurance to provide for yourself and others in any emergency. Always take out insurance against an emergency that you cannot write a check to cover. Insure your car for liability and collision. Insure your health for unexpected setbacks, and insure your life so that if something unfortunate happens to you, the people who are counting on you will be provided for. One of the deepest needs of human nature is the desire for security. Without insurance, your life is simply a gamble, which can cause you stress and unhappiness.

The third part of the law of three says that you should invest 10 to 20 percent of your income throughout your life until your investments earn more than you do.

Your life is divided into roughly three parts, although they tend to overlap. First, there are your learning years, where you grow up and get your education. Then there are your earning years, from approximately twenty years to approximately sixty-five years of age. After that come your yearning years, when you can retire. (In 2023, the average U.S. life expectancy was 79.11 years.)

The simplest and most effective financial strategy is to save and invest your money continually until it is paying you more than you earn at your job. At that point, you can begin to phase out of your job and phase in to managing your assets.

This seems like a very simple lifetime planning strategy, but it's remarkable how few people follow it and how many people end up at the age of sixty-five with very little put aside.

The Law of Investing

The ninth law of money is the *law of investing*. This law states that you should investigate before you invest. You should spend at least as much time studying a particular investment as you do earning the money to put into it. Never let yourself be rushed into parting with money that you've worked so hard for and taken so long to accumulate. Investigate every single aspect of the investment before you make any commitment. Ask for full and complete disclosure— for honest, accurate, and adequate information. If you have any doubt or misgivings, you'll probably be far better off keeping your money in a tax-deferred savings or money market investment than you would be taking the risk of losing it.

The first part of the law of investing is that the only thing easy about money is losing it. It's very hard to make money in a competitive society, but losing it is one of the easiest things you can ever do. A Japanese proverb says that making money is like digging with a nail, whereas losing money is like pouring water on the sand.

Making money is like digging with a nail, whereas losing money is like pouring water on the sand.

The second part of this law comes from the self-made billionaire Marvin Davis, who was asked about his rules regarding money in a 1989 *Forbes* magazine interview. He said that he has one simple rule: don't lose money. If there's a possibility that you'll lose your money, don't part with it in the first place. This principle is so important that you should write it down and repeat it over and over.

The third part of the law of investing says that if you think you can afford to lose a little, you're going to end up losing a lot. There's something about the attitude of a person who feels they have enough money that they can afford to risk losing a little. You remember the old saying, "A fool and his money are soon parted." There's another saying: when a man with experience meets a man with money, the man with the money is going to end up with some experience and the man with experience is going to end up with the money.

The fourth part of the law of investing says to only invest with experts who have a proven track record of success in handling money. I once had dinner with a man in Portland, Oregon, who had started with nothing and gradually worked his way up to being worth several million dollars. He had a simple philosophy: he would only invest with people who were doing better than he was with their own money.

Because this man was a successful investor, he was often approached by people selling investments of various kinds. He would always tell the seller that he was willing to trade personal financial statements. If the seller would show him his personal financial statement, he would show the seller his. If the seller was doing better than he was, he would accept the seller's advice and buy the investment. But if he was doing better than the seller, he would decline. Most people who approached this man for investment funds were not doing well at all. They would leave quietly and never come back.

Your job is to invest only with people who have such a successful track record that your risk is dramatically diminished. Don't lose money. If ever you feel tempted. refer back to this rule and hold on to what you have.

The Law of Compound Interest

The tenth law of money is the *law of compound interest*. It states that investing your money carefully and allowing it to grow at compound interest will eventually make you rich. When you let money accumulate at compound interest tax-free, it can grow more rapidly than you can imagine.

You can use the rule of 72 to determine how long it will take for your money to double by dividing the interest rate into the number 72. For example, if you were receiving 8 percent interest on your investment or your savings, you would divide the number 72 by 8, and you'd come out with 9. This means it would take you 9 years to double your money at 8 percent interest. Of course, the more money you add to the account, the faster it will grow, but the rule of 72 applies to any interest rate.

The first part of the law of compound interest says $1 invested at 3 percent interest at the time of Christ would be worth half the money in the world today. If the money had been allowed to grow and double and then double again and again, it would be worth billions or trillions of dollars today.

This brings us to the second part of this law, which says that the key to compound interest is to put your money away and never touch it.

The Law of Accumulation

Eleventh is the *law of accumulation*, which says that every great financial achievement is an accumulation of hundreds and thousands of small efforts and sacrifices that no one ever sees or appreciates. When you begin moving toward financial independence, it'll require a tremendous number of small efforts on your part. To begin this process, you must be disciplined and persistent. You must keep at it for a long, long time. Eventually your efforts will begin to bear fruit. In just a little while, you'll begin to pull ahead of your peers, and by developing a long time perspective, you can virtually assure that you'll end up rich.

The first part of the law of accumulation says that as you accumulate savings, you develop a momentum that moves you more rapidly towards your goal. Once you begin saving, you begin to develop a rate of momentum that's very important for you to maintain. It's hard to get started on a program of financial accumulation, but once you do, you need to keep at it continually. If ever you allow yourself to lose the momentum and slow to a halt, it becomes extremely difficult to start up again. Momentum is one of the secrets of success that you need to develop and maintain in everything you do.

The second part of this law comes from the late Reverend Robert Schuller, who said that by the yard, it's hard, but inch by inch, anything's a cinch. When we talk about saving 10 or 20 percent of your income, most people are initially overwhelmed and disappointed. They're already up to their necks in debt and bills, and they're spending every single penny that they earn just to keep afloat. If you find yourself in this situation, you can begin saving just 1 percent of your income in a special account, which you refuse to touch. Begin putting your change into a large jar every evening when you come home. When the jar is full, take it to the bank and add it to your savings account. Whenever you get an extra sum of money from selling something or an old debt is repaid or you receive an unexpected bonus, instead of spending it, put it into a savings account, it'll start to add up at a rate that might surprise you. As you become comfortable with saving 1 percent, move it up to 2 percent, then 3 percent, then 4 percent and 5 percent, and so on. Within a year, you'll find yourself getting out of debt and saving 10, 15, and even 20 percent of your income without really affecting your lifestyle.

The Law of Attraction

The twelfth law of money is the *law of attraction*, which I've mentioned before in a different context. In this context, it says that as you begin accumulating money, by magnetizing it with the emotion of desire, you will begin to attract even more money to yourself.

The first part of this law as applied to money is that a prosperity consciousness—one that works and prepares for and expects prosperity—attracts money like iron filings to a magnet. When I first read about the importance of developing a prosperity consciousness, I was broke and in my early twenties. I didn't fully understand what it meant. It sounded good, but I didn't know how to do it.

Prosperity consciousness attracts money like iron filings to a magnet.

Over the years, however, I found that as you develop a positive and expectant attitude toward money and you begin believing in the law of abundance, your emotions somehow magnetize the money that you've saved, and you begin to attract more of it into your life.

The second part of this law is something that you've heard before: it takes money to make money. As you begin accumulating money, you begin to attract more money and more opportunities to earn even more. This is why it's so important to start even with a small amount; you'll be amazed at what happens.

The Law of Accelerating Acceleration

The thirteenth law of money is the *law of accelerating acceleration*, which says that as you begin moving toward your goal of financial freedom, it begins moving toward you at an accelerating speed.

The first part of this law is that nothing succeeds like success. The more money and success you achieve, the more money and success seem to move towards you from a variety of directions. Everyone who's financially successful today has had the experience of working extremely hard before they got their first real opportunity. However, after that, more and more opportunities began to flow to them like a river, and their major problem today is sorting out their opportunities to increase their money and improve their well-being. It'll be the same for you.

The second part of the law of accelerating acceleration says that 80 percent of your success will come in the last 20 percent of the time you put in. This remarkable discovery says that you'll achieve only about 20 percent of the total success possible for you in the first 80 percent of the time and money that you invest; you will achieve the other 80 percent in the last 20 percent of the time and money that you invest. Peter Lynch, the legendary manager of the Magellan mutual funds (which were among the most successful mutual funds in history), said that the best investments he ever made were those that took the longest time to come to fruition. He would often buy the stock of a company that didn't increase in value for several years and then went up ten or twenty times in price. This strategy of picking stocks for the long term eventually made him one of the highest-paid money managers in America.

A simple way to prove this truth to yourself is to take a penny and double it every day for thirty days. On the first day, you'll have 1 cent. On the second day, you'll have 2 cents. On the third day, you'll have 4 cents, then 8 cents, then 16 cents, then 32 cents, and so on. By the thirtieth day, you'll have several million dollars. However, on the twenty-ninth day, you'll have only half of the amount that you'll have on the thirtieth day, and on the twenty-eighth day, you'll have only one quarter of what you'll have on the thirtieth day. Don't make the mistake of pulling out too soon and giving up all of the great increase that's possible if you wait.

The laws of money say that starting wherever you are—even deeply in debt or working for someone else, even if you haven't been serious about money in the past—you can save your money, invest it carefully, get out of debt, and achieve your financial goals. The only real question you have to ask with regard to money is, how badly do you want it? You're always free to choose. You are responsible. No one is ever going to do it for you. It's always up to you, but if you decide to follow these laws and principles and if you persist long enough and hard enough, there is virtually nothing that can stop you from achieving financial success.

The Laws of Money

The law of abundance. There is an ample supply of money for everyone who really wants it and who obeys the laws of cause and effect as they apply to money.

The law of exchange. Money is the medium through which people exchange their production of goods and services for the goods and services of others.

The law of capital. Your most valuable asset is your physical and mental capital, your earning ability.

The law of time perspective. The most successful people are those who take the longest time period into consideration when making their day-to-day decisions.

The law of saving. Financial freedom comes to individuals who save 10 percent or more of their income throughout their lifetime.

The law of conservation. It's not how much you make but how much you keep that will determine your financial future.

Parkinson's law. Expenses always rise to meet income.

The law of three. There are three legs to the stool of financial freedom: savings, insurance, and investment.

The law of investing. Investigate before you invest. Spend at least as much time studying a particular investment as you do earning the money to put into it.

The law of compound interest. Investing your money carefully and allowing it to grow at compound interest will eventually make you rich.

The law of accumulation. Every great financial achievement is an accumulation of hundreds and thousands of small efforts and sacrifices that no one ever sees or appreciates.

The law of attraction. As you begin accumulating money, by magnetizing it with the emotion of desire, you will attract even more money to yourself.

The law of accelerating acceleration. As you begin moving toward your goal of financial freedom, it begins moving toward you at an accelerating speed.

eight

The Laws of Wealth Creation

There are more wealthy men and women in America than in any other nation, and the number is growing at a steady pace. As of late 2023, there were nearly 22 million millionaires in this country: 40 percent of the world's total, according to *Forbes*. In 2021, America gained 2.5 million new millionaires. As of April 2023, the total number of global billionaires was 2,544,756 of which were in the United States.

Now here are a couple of questions for you. First, do you sincerely want to be rich? If you do, you must be willing to pay the price in terms of effort and sacrifice over a long time—probably more than twenty years—in order to achieve it. If you're not willing to pay this kind of a price, you don't really want to be rich. You're merely entertaining yourself with a fantasy.

The second question is this: if you sincerely want to be rich, why aren't you? What is stopping you? Is it your income or the rate of your spending? When I talked about the laws of money, I covered many of the key principles that you must apply to achieve financial independence, but if you want to be rich, you have to go much further.

Theoretically, it's possible for you or anyone else to become rich, to achieve a net worth in excess of $1 million during the course of your working lifetime. All you have to do is to begin saving early enough, continue it long enough, shelter your savings from taxes as much as possible, and let your wealth build up until it passes the million-dollar mark. Virtually anyone can do it, and hundreds of thousands of people are doing it right now.

Having worked with hundreds of corporations and many tens of thousands of individuals, I've met hundreds of millionaires and several billionaires. I've found that they're not very different from you and me, aside from the fact that they have more money and, as they say, a better class of problems. They're no more intelligent, nor are they especially gifted. They are mostly ordinary men and women who have used their God-given abilities to an extraordinary degree in their chosen fields. They've developed themselves and their opportunities to a very high point, and nothing in this world can stop you from joining them if you really want to.

I've already discussed the law of belief, which says that your beliefs become your realities. Thoughts objectify themselves; the thoughts held in your mind produce after their kind. What you really deeply and intensely believe tends to materialize in your experience. Your beliefs cause you to think, see, feel, and behave in ways that tend to make your beliefs come true for you.

Thoughts objectify themselves; the thoughts held in your mind produce after their kind.

When I was in my teens, even though I came from a poor background, I had a dream of being a millionaire by the time I was thirty. Like most people, I traveled, worked, and tried many things during my twenties. I switched back and forth, searching for that elusive will-o'-the-wisp of financial riches. I eagerly looked for lucky breaks, and I tried various get-rich-quick schemes. I threw my heart and energy into a variety of enterprises, looking for a fast way to reach that million-dollar mark.

I didn't make it. When I was thirty, I was deeply in debt, between jobs once more, and I didn't even have a high school diploma. As my thirties began, I set my goal to be a millionaire by the time I was forty. I began to draw on my experience and do a few things right, but the idea of achieving wealth was still just a dream.

Then there came a turning point in my life. I'd been working very hard in business—still with a dream of someday becoming wealthy—when someone asked me to explain the qualities of self-made millionaires. As I considered the question, all I could come up with were some platitudes about setting goals and working hard. This awareness of my own ignorance led me to begin studying men and women who had started from nothing and achieved financial independence, and here is where the law of belief came to work for me. It can do the same for you.

I found that there was an enormous amount of information available on the rich. Apparently the subject had fascinated many people before me. This is when my beliefs began to grow. Think about it: if you read one book about one person who had started from pretty much the same place you did and had become wealthy because of doing certain things in a certain way, you would develop at least a small belief that it might be possible for you.

If you went on to read about ten or 100 or 1,000 men and women who had started with very little and had worked their way up to wealth and prestige, your belief would begin to deepen and intensify to the point where you could become convinced that you too had the capacity to achieve whatever financial goals you set for yourself.

That's what happened to me. As I began studying wealthy Americans and especially self-made millionaires, not only did I learn the cause and effect relationships, the things that they'd done to get where they were, but I also began to develop the belief that it was possible for me as well. My intensity of belief activated the law of attraction within me and began drawing into my life people, circumstances, ideas, and resources that began to move me toward my financial goals and to move them toward me. All of the other laws of success and achievement that I'm discussing in this book began to work on my behalf. In just a few years I was able to go from being broke to being financially independent. As I began sharing these ideas with others, they began to go from rags to riches as well.

All over the country men and women have found that by applying some of these principles, they can make more progress in a couple of years than they might have made in an entire lifetime of hard work.

There is a series of laws that apply to wealth creation and which you can use to achieve your financial goals. Every wealthy person lives in harmony with these laws, and every person suffering financial problems is breaking one or more of these laws and trying to get away with it. Unfortunately, it just doesn't work that way.

The Law of Creative Emulation

The first law of wealth creation is the *law of creative emulation*. It says that the key to achieving wealth is to study and emulate those who have already acquired it before you. Don't try to reinvent the wheel; use proven success methods.

The first part of this law says that what one person has done others can do as well. Abraham Lincoln once said that some become wealthy is a sign to others that they may also become wealthy. For every activity, it's commonly understood that you copy the people who have already mastered the subject before you attempt to add your own variations to it.

The second part of the law of creative emulation says that if you ask the experts for advice, they'll give it to you. The late business philosopher Jim Rohn said that poor people should take rich people out to lunch and pay the bill. Taking a wealthy, successful person out to lunch and asking them for guidance on what you can do and how you can do it is the cheapest investment you can ever make, and I've found that winners will always help others to win. Successful people will always take time out of their busy schedules to help other people to be successful.

The third part of the law of creative emulation says that you become what you most admire. Wealthy men and women place an extremely high value on the acquisition of material goods, and they very much admire and look up to others who have acquired them as well. Sometimes people delude themselves by saying silly things like, "I'd rather be happy than rich." They seem to think that people who make a lot of money are not particularly virtuous or happy. Well, I have news for you. The research has been done, and the results are in: the wealthy are very happy. They may have problems and difficulties, but they are happier and healthier more of the time than people who worry about money every day.

Many people have been misled into believing that one only achieves financial success by engaging in activities that are somehow illicit and unacceptable. This is disproven by the facts. More than 99 percent of all the men and women who have achieved wealth have done it by utilizing their talents and abilities to the maximum in the service of other people. The biggest fortunes in America have been built in fields like retail sales, food production and distribution, gasoline and oil distribution, real estate development, and transportation of people, goods, and services. Many huge fortunes come from the development of media outlets like newspapers, television, radio stations, and more recently the Internet. The way to wealth is summarized in the old saying, "If you want to dine with the classes, you have to sell to the masses."

The Law of Desire

The second law of wealth creation is the *law of desire*, which states that the motivation to acquire riches is an intense, burning desire for financial success. In order to achieve anything, you must be highly motivated, and all motivation requires a motive. The more powerful your motivation, the more likely you are to persist in the face of obstacles and disappointments.

The first part of the law of desire says that if you want something badly enough, no one will be able to convince you that it's not possible. The greatest negative influence in your life may be the people around you, many of them well-meaning, who will criticize and ridicule you for wanting to achieve so much above the ordinary. They'll point out every weakness and shortcoming in your plans and dreams, but if your desire is intense enough, you'll be able to rise above them and carry on regardless.

If you want something badly enough, no one will be able to convince you that it's not possible.

The second part of the law of desire says that desire is expressed only in your actions. It's not what you say, but what you do that counts. As I've already indicated, everybody has the same dreams and desires, but very few people take actions consistent with them. You can tell if you really believe in your ability to become wealthy by the things that you do every day. The wonderful thing is that when you take actions consistent with your desires, the actions themselves reinforce your belief that your desires are achievable. You can build yourself into an unstoppable human wealth creating machine by acting as if you already are one.

The third part of the law of desire says that the more often you affirm your goal and visualize it as a reality, the more intense your desire will be.

The Law of Purpose

The third law of wealth creation is the *law of purpose*. As Napoleon Hill said, "definiteness of purpose is the starting point of all riches." Definiteness of purpose means establishing a clear, well-defined goal of financial achievement for yourself, supported by a plan and backed by action. Setting wealth creation as your major definite purpose in life is essential to turning it into a reality.

The first part of the law of purpose says that a person with a clear purpose will make progress on the roughest road. If you know exactly where you're going, you'll find a way to get there. It doesn't matter how difficult the way or how many obstacles you face: as long as your goal is clear, you'll find a way under, over, or around anything that blocks your path.

Here's an exercise that will start you on your way. Take a pad of paper, write down some clear financial goals for yourself, and make a plan that extends out over the next three to five years. Draw up a list of everything you can think of that you can do to begin your forward movement. Organize the list in terms of priorities, and begin to work on the item that appears most important to you. Decide how much you want to earn each year, how much you plan to save and invest, how much you want to be worth when you retire, and how much of an annual return you want to earn on your accumulated savings. The more definite you are, the more likely it is that these numbers will become your reality.

The second part of the law of purpose says that many people fail to become rich, first, because it never occurs to them, and second, they never decide to. They never even think about it, so be careful with whom you associate on a regular basis. You'll inevitably adopt the mannerisms, values, attitudes, and behaviors of the people with whom you spend the most time, even if it does occur to you that it would be nice to be wealthy.

The second major obstacle to financial success is that most people never decide to accomplish it. They wish and hope and pray and buy lottery tickets, but they never make a total, 100 percent commitment to paying the price of success in advance so that they can enjoy it in the future.

There are some beautiful words attributed (although incorrectly) to the German poet and philosopher Johann Wolfgang von Goethe. Here is one version: "Whatever you can do, or dream you can do, begin it. Boldness has genius, power, and magic in it!"

The Law of Enrichment

The fourth law of wealth creation is the *law of enrichment*, which says that all lasting wealth comes from enriching others in some way—from adding value and retaining part of it. This law says that anyone who enriches others must themselves be enriched. Since the world is full of men and women driven by expediency to get the very most for the very least of the security, comfort, leisure, love, respect, and fulfillment that they want, there are unlimited opportunities to enrich the lives of others. All you have to do is find your own particular way and then manage your affairs so that you keep a small part of the value that you've added to the life and work of other people.

The law of enrichment goes on to say that your current income is a measure of how much you are currently enriching the lives of others. You are paid not what you want but what you deserve. You're earning today exactly what you're worth—not a penny more, not a penny less. What you're being paid at this moment represents exactly how much value your efforts represent in the lives of the people who use what you produce. You can only increase the amount that you are getting by increasing the amount that you're giving.

The Law of Entrepreneurship

The fifth law of wealth creation is the *law of entrepreneurship*: more people become wealthy by starting and building their own successful businesses than by all other ways combined. A CNBC story from February 2023 indicated that 51 percent of millionaires were entrepreneurs, 28 percent had traditional nine-to-five jobs, and 18 percent were senior executives at large companies.

Fully 74 percent of self-made millionaires in the United States achieve their wealth by starting a business enterprise and building it up, usually very slowly, so that it not only yielded them a good living but generated enough excess revenue to eventually make them wealthy.

The first part of the law of entrepreneurship simply says, find a need and fill it: this has been the essence of all business success, large and small. Look around you, find a need that people have, and find a way to fill it in a cost-effective manner.

Find a need and fill it: this has been the essence of all business success.

The second part of the law of entrepreneurship says that wherever there are needs unmet or problems unsolved, there are opportunities to create wealth.

The third part of the law says that most fortunes come from selling established products or services in established markets to established customers, but doing it just a little bit better. A product or service has to be only 10 percent newer or better to create a business and start a fortune.

The converse of this principle is that it's very risky to start off with an unproven or untried product or service. The industry that's produced more self-made millionaires than any other single industry is the dry-cleaning business. This is because dry cleaning is an established service need that's used regularly. It's fairly profitable, and it's required by almost everyone.

It's not impossible to make money with a brand-new product or service, but it's a little like hoping for a miracle. Miracles do happen, but you can't depend upon them. More people lose their shirts and their hopes by trying to sell something brand-new in a brand-new market than by any other way.

The Law of Bootstrapping

Sixth is the *law of bootstrapping*. This law states that entrepreneurs who start with too little capital are usually more successful than those who start with too much. You've probably heard that most businesses fail because they don't have enough capital; they run out of money. The fact of the matter is probably that more businesses fail because they start off with too much money rather than too little. The reason is simple: the most valuable thing an entrepreneur can bring to a new business idea is energy and imagination. When you have very little money, you have to use your intelligence and your efforts as substitutes. You don't have the luxury of using money to smooth out the bumps or put a cushion under you. When you're down to your last dollar or starting off with virtually no money at all, you develop street smarts. You learn how to think on your feet and act quickly.

Some of the smartest and most successful businesspeople have used bootstrapping as the key method of achieving their goals. Many people hold back from starting a business because they're convinced that they need a lot of money. When they go to a bank, they're turned down. But banks don't lend money for business start-ups. Banks are in the business of making good loans, that is, loans to people who can back the money that they are borrowing with $2, $3, $4, or $5 for every dollar they're asking the bank to lend. If you don't have that, the bank won't even talk to you. As for venture capitalists, fully 99 percent of all proposals put into the hands of venture capitalists are turned down, and many of the 1 percent that are backed fail as well.

Most businesses are built up by bootstrapping and by "love money": money that people lend or give to you because they love you. Most entrepreneurs finance their own startups or finance them with money from their parents, family members, or friends. This is the most common way of getting a business going in America today.

I have already mentioned the first part of the law of bootstrapping: the most important resources in a new business are energy and imagination. If you have enough energy and imagination, you'll ultimately triumph, no matter what happens in the short term. On the other hand, if you lack energy and imagination, you can go through any amount of money and you'll ultimately fail. Consequently, the sooner you develop your street smarts (which depends upon your having very little money to start with), the faster you'll be successful.

The second part of this law says that skill, knowledge, and experience develop in inverse proportion to the amount of capital available. The less capital you have, the smarter you get and the more likely you are to succeed.

The Law of Courage

The seventh law of wealth creation is the *law of courage*, which says that your willingness to risk failure and disappointment is a measure of your desire to be rich.

Your willingness to risk failure and disappointment is a measure of your desire to be rich.

The first part of this law says, no guts, no glory. You've got to be willing to stick your neck out. If you want to lift your head above the crowd, you have to go out on a limb, because that's where the fruit of life is.

The second part of the law of courage says that there is nothing to fear but fear itself. This was first said by President Franklin D. Roosevelt during the Great Depression, and it's just as true today.

One of the best ways to deal with fear is to ask yourself, what's the worst thing that can possibly happen? Most of your fear comes from failing to identify the worst possible consequences of your situation. Once you've clearly defined what might happen, you can do everything to make sure that it doesn't.

The third part of the law of courage says, do the thing you fear, and the death of fear is certain. Confronting your fears and moving ahead despite them is the way to develop the courage that's essential to long-term success. Dare to go forward. Winston Churchill once said, "Courage is rightly considered the foremost of the virtues, for upon it all others depend."

The Law of Risk

Eighth is the *law of risk*: there is a direct relationship between the level of risk and the likelihood of loss. In fact, risk *is* the likelihood of loss. People who become wealthy are extremely astute at assessing the level of risk in every situation. They carefully analyze the ratio of risk to return before deciding to invest their time or money.

Begin your analysis by realizing that a perfectly safe investment in a money market or savings account can yield between 4 and 5 percent interest (which are the best rates as of late 2023). If you're going to invest your time and money, you must be assured of a return that is substantially higher in order to compensate you for the possibility of loss.

When you assess the risk, include all the possible costs; include your labor at your desired hourly rate as an investment as well.

Many entrepreneurs think they're doing well because they don't count their own labor as a cost of doing business. You value your own labor by determining how much you would be paid if you went to work for another company and counting that as a cost of doing business. You also take the money that you have tied up in the business and calculate what you'd earn on it at a safe rate of return. This is called an *opportunity cost*, which, combined with your opportunity cost of labor, will show you the real level of your investment and risk.

The first part of the law of risk comes from the late publisher Malcolm Forbes, who said, "If it sounds too good to be true, it probably is." One of the greatest wastes of time, life, and money is the pursuit of get-rich-quick schemes, which seem to come down the pipeline with astonishing regularity. The only real way to get rich dependably is to get rich slowly. It's hard work, and it takes a long time to accumulate wealth, but you're foolish to seek for faster and easier ways.

The only real way to get rich dependably is to get rich slowly.

The second part of this law says that success in wealth creation is the result of avoiding risk in the pursuit of profit. Entrepreneurs are not risk takers, as is commonly believed; they are risk avoiders. They're skillful at sidestepping risk in the pursuit of adding value and earning profits. It's only to the degree to which you avoid the risks inherent in any economic activity that you become wealthy.

The third part of the law of risk says that entrepreneurs take calculated risks, but they are not gamblers. Extensive research on the behavior of successful entrepreneurs shows that because they work hard for their money, they have no desire to gamble it away. They accept that there's a certain amount of risk in anything they do, but they believe they can tip the scales to their own advantage. They can moderate the risk by adding their knowledge, skills, and ability to the equation. They are willing to take gambles only when they can personally have an effect on the outcome. You seldom see entrepreneurs in gambling resorts or trading in the stock market. If they're in the stock market at all, they have investment portfolios where they store their excess funds for the long term. Their funds are carefully allocated among blue-chip stocks and are supervised by professional money managers. If you ask the average self-made millionaire how the stock market did today, he will tell you quite frankly that he doesn't know. They don't follow the stock market, because they're not interested in day-to-day fluctuations.

The Law of Undue Optimism

The ninth law of wealth creation is called *the law of undue optimism*, and it's essential for both entrepreneurship and the creation of wealth. It says, an unwarranted expectancy of success can lead to both success and failure. Excess optimism is essential for a person to embark on a new business adventure. Without undue optimism, without an extremely positive feeling that you'll be successful, you'll tend to play it too safe, as most people do. To get started in the first place, you need an attitude of hopefulness and positive expectancy that is much higher than average.

Yet this same undue optimism can lead to self-delusion and unreal expectations, so you need to temper optimism with reality. Examine every aspect of the business before you commit your resources. Seek out the advice of other people who may not be as positive towards your idea as you are, and carefully consider what they say before you act.

The first part of this law says that the true time period for you to break even will be three times longer than your best estimate. Once you've written out your business plan, triple your best estimate of your break-even point and make sure you have the resources to continue operating that long. When starting on any new venture, practice frugality at all times, and conserve your cash above all else.

The second part of the law of undue optimism is that whatever your budget is for your venture, it will cost you twice as much as you expect. So be conservative in projecting your sales and revenues, and be liberal, even excessive, in estimating your costs. Always calculate your expenses on the outside, at the highest you can imagine. When you have them all added up, add another 20 percent as a fudge factor to get a more realistic picture of your likely costs. If you exceed your financial expectations, that's wonderful, but practice caution and pessimism in your projections.

The third part of the law of undue optimism is called Murphy's law, which, as we've already seen, says that whatever can go wrong *will* go wrong. A corollary says that of all the possible things that can go wrong, the worst possible thing will go wrong at the worst possible time, and it will cost the greatest amount of money.

People who start their own businesses are convinced (at least initially) that they're going to violate these laws and succeed in spite of them. People who succeed, however, conform to these laws and have stopped trying to beat them.

The Law of Persistence

This, the tenth law, says that if you persist long enough, you must inevitably be successful. Persistence is to an individual as carbon is to steel. Your persistence is your measure of your belief in yourself. It is your self-discipline in action, and it's often your most valuable asset.

The first part of the law of persistence says that the entire process of wealth creation is just one important lesson after another. If ever you feel that you reach the point where you know everything you need to know, in no time at all you're going to be blindsided by a completely new and unexpected series of problems and difficulties.

The second part of the law of persistence says that you stay in business and achieve success only as long as you continue to earn enough money to pay for your mistakes. The freedom to fail gives you the opportunity to succeed. You are learning all the time. When you have experiences, either positive or negative, you'll learn from them, and what you learn will enable you to win in the end.

By the law of accumulation, your ultimate success will be an accumulation of hundreds and even thousands of small actions on your part that gradually add up to a critical mass that enables you to create and keep wealth.

Perhaps the most important thing you can do is take time every day to think about your goals and reflect quietly on what you've done right and what you would do differently in the future. Action without thinking is the cause of every failure.

Wealth is within your grasp. Hundreds of thousands of men and women have acquired it in the past, and you can acquire it if you do the same things and learn the same lessons they did. The only real limitation on your potential is the level of your desire and your willingness to persist in the face of adversity. When you set a clear goal, develop a written plan, put your plan into action, and back your actions with determination and perseverance, you must and will eventually succeed. You will become one of the leading men or women of your generation.

The Laws of Wealth Creation

The law of creative emulation. The key to achieving wealth is to study and emulate those who have already acquired it.

The law of desire. The motivation to acquire riches is an intense, burning desire for financial success.

The law of purpose. Definiteness of purpose is the starting point of all riches. Definiteness of purpose means establishing a clear, well-defined goal of financial achievement for yourself, supported by a plan and backed by action.

The law of enrichment. All lasting wealth comes from enriching others in some way—from adding value and retaining part of it.

The law of entrepreneurship. More people become wealthy by starting and building their own successful businesses than by all other ways combined.

The law of bootstrapping. Entrepreneurs who start with too little capital are usually more successful than those who start with too much.

The law of courage. Your willingness to risk failure and disappointment is a measure of your desire to be rich.

The law of risk. There is a direct relationship between the level of risk and the likelihood of loss.

The law of undue optimism. An unwarranted expectancy of success can lead to both the success and failure of a new business venture.

The law of persistence. If you persist long enough, you must inevitably succeed.

nine

The Laws of Sales

Everyone makes their living selling something to someone. Everyone is paid both tangibly and intangibly on the basis of how well they sell themselves and their ideas, products, and services to others. It's not a matter of *whether* you sell or not. It's only a matter of how good you are at it. Parents, for example, are continually selling values, attitudes, and behaviors to their children, and their children will grow up straight and strong to the degree to which the parents have been good at this job. The best managers and leaders are invariably described as excellent low-pressure salespeople. Since people don't like to be told, taught, or talked down to, the most successful human relations experts are those who can present an idea in such a way that the other person will embrace it as their own.

President Dwight D. Eisenhower once said that the art of leadership is getting people to do what you want them to do and think of it as their own idea. You are paid largely for your ability to sell the quality of your work to the people who determine your career success. Many people market themselves aggressively and effectively in their careers, and they move ahead far more rapidly than others who don't, even though they may not be more talented or producing more or better work; it's all in the selling. Many people (including many salespeople) are uneasy about the word *selling*, yet the ability to persuade and influence others is central to a happy life.

The opposite to influencing and persuading others is having no ability to influence or persuade—to be merely a passive agent in the flow of events. People who can't get others to go along with them have very little influence and are little respected. People who have developed the ability to be persuasive and convincing are some of the most respected and successful people in our society.

The ability to sell well is one of the rarest talents in America. Top salespeople are some of the best-paid, most respected, and most secure of all professionals, so whether you are a customer, a manager, a salesperson, or anyone else, you owe it to yourself to become excellent at selling whatever you sell to other people.

To speak specifically of the sales profession, the Pareto principle applies: roughly 80 percent of consequences come from 20 percent of causes. Hence the top 20 percent of salespeople sell 80 percent of the business and earn 80 percent of the money. Research shows that the top 10 percent of salespeople open 80 percent of the new accounts and are some of the highest-paid people in the business world.

Today there's more research available on selling effectively than at any other time in history. We know more about how to succeed in selling than ever before, and that's what we'll cover in this chapter.

Selling involves three essential factors: (1) the product or service, (2) the salesperson, and (3) the customer. All three must be ideally suited to one another for a sale to take place.

Let me explain. The product or service must be right for the customer, but it also must be right for the salesperson. Some salespeople are excellent at selling one type of product or service, and some are excellent at another. It has very little to do with the product itself. It often has to do with the temperament, personality, values, and attitude of the salesperson. It's hard to sell something that you can't put your whole heart into. Many people have found by changing products or services, they've gone to the top of their industries, whereas before they were merely spinning their wheels.

The starting point of sales success, then, is to make sure that these three factors are in place: this is the right product or service for you to be selling to the right customer, the one you most enjoy working with.

The thirteen laws that you can use to become far more effective and successful in sales.

The Law of Sales

The first is the *law of sales*, which says nothing happens until a sale takes place. These words come from the great salesman and sales trainer Red Motley: a sale initiates the entire production process. It activates the factories and provides employment for the workers. It pays salaries and wages. It pays taxes and dividends, and it determines the entire direction of society. Whenever sales are good, the economy is strong and full of opportunities for growth and prosperity. Sales levels are the first thing to slow down when the economy begins to soften.

Nothing happens until a sale takes place.

The first part of the law of sales says that products and services are sold, not bought. No matter how good a product or service is, in a competitive market and with customers who are busy and preoccupied, products and services must ultimately be sold, and they require someone to sell them. The skill of selling is therefore one guarantor of a happy and prosperous life.

The second part of this law says that customers need to be *asked* to buy. No matter how much a customer likes you or your product, there's always a certain amount of indecision or hesitation at the point of buying, and it's the job of the salesperson to help the customer through this difficult moment into the enjoyment of owning and using the product or service.

The third part of this law says that 80 percent of sales are closed after the fifth call or the fifth closing attempt. In complex sales, which are sales involving several people in several meetings with a client, most sales are closed after the fifth meeting or interaction. In simple sales, which are sales requiring only a single meeting with a client or customer, most sales are closed after the fifth time that the salesperson asks the customer to make a buying decision. It's therefore essential that the salesperson plans the close of the sales conversation in advance and has a variety of different ways to ask for the order.

The fourth part of this law says that 50 percent of salespeople quit after the first call in a complex sale, and 50 percent of salespeople fail to ask for the order even once in a simple sale.

For example, a sales organization I worked with sent out consultants with their salespeople and found that they were asking for the order an average of four times per sales conversation, and their sales weren't very high. They taught the salespeople to ask for the order at least five times in each conversation, and their sales doubled within the next thirty days. Often, each time you ask a customer to decide, the customer draws closer to making the final decision. Sadly, many salespeople quit when the sale is just within reach by failing to ask for the order one more time.

The fifth part of the law of sales comes from the New Testament, which says, "Ask and you shall receive." There's no miracle to success in selling. Top salespeople just see more people and ask more often. If you want to join the top ranks of sales professionals, you must simply increase your frequency of contact with your customers.

Let me tell you another story: A large company in California paid many thousands of dollars to bring in an outside consulting firm to find out why their sales were down. They found that their salespeople had begun to drift in their sales activities and were only making four customer contacts per week. Immediately upon discovering this, the company instituted a control procedure which required that each salesperson meet face-to-face with at least ten customers per week. Their sales jumped 50 percent during the first month. They proved again that no amount of training or skill can replace the need to get knee to knee with customers.

The Law of Ambition

The second law of selling is the *law of ambition*, which says how high you rise is largely determined by how high you want to climb. How far you go in your field and how much money you earn are not determined solely by external factors; they're determined more by internal factors—by your level of desire and ambition.

The first part of the law of ambition says, commit to being the best in your field. The commitment to excellence will propel you onward and upward and assure you of great success. All top sales-people got to their place only after they'd firmly decided to be the best at what they were doing.

The second part of the law of ambition says that to achieve high sales goals, you have to set them in the first place. The starting point of great success in selling is to decide how much you want to earn each year and how much you're going to have to sell in order to earn it.

Break your annual sales goals down into monthly, weekly, and even daily goals. Then divide your annual income goal by the number 250, which represents the number of working days in an average year, to determine how much you want to earn each day. Divide your daily earnings goal by 8 to determine how much you want to earn per hour. From that moment onward, never do anything that doesn't pay you your desired hourly rate. For example, if you want to earn $250,000 a year, dividing that number by 250 would give you $1,000 per day or $125 per hour for an eight-hour day. From then on, never do anything that you wouldn't pay someone else $125 per hour to do. Don't even drop off your dry cleaning or pick up your groceries or socialize on the telephone. These activities don't pay $125 per hour, and if you don't do $125 per hour work eight hours a day, it's impossible, by the law of cause and effect, ever to earn $50,000 per year.

That's why all top salespeople are extremely well disciplined in the way they use their time, hour by hour, throughout the working day.

The third part of the law of ambition says that you can't fly with the eagles if you continue to scratch with the turkeys (this line comes from Zig Ziglar). In order to be the best in your field, you must associate with the best people in your field. At the same time, you must get away from the 80 percent of salespeople who are going nowhere.

Most top salespeople tend to be loners: they find that in order to keep themselves positive, motivated, and focused, they've got to stay away from the great majority of other salespeople, who are not. Discipline yourself in this area. If you want to be a top salesperson, get around other top salespeople.

The Law of Need

Third is the *law of need*, which says that every decision to purchase a product or service is an attempt to satisfy a need or relieve a dissatisfaction. One of the most important things you do in successful selling is to put yourself in the shoes of your prospect and see your offering through their eyes.

The first part of the law of need says that before selling anything to anyone, the salesperson must be clear about the need that they are attempting to satisfy. Good salespeople are very good at asking questions and listening intently to the answers. This enables them to focus in on satisfying the customer's most important and pressing needs with their product or service.

The second part of the law of need says that sales success comes from fulfilling existing needs, not creating new ones. Your job is to uncover the needs that already exist, not to attempt to convince a person that they have needs that they may not have thought of in the first place.

The third part of this law says that the more basic the need, the more basic the sales presentation. If you're selling potatoes, which caters to the need for food, you can sell them very simply: by size and weight. Your sales appeal will be to appetite and attractiveness.

Your basis of comparison with other foodstuffs will be simple and straightforward.

Correspondingly, the fourth part of this law says that the more complex the need, the more sophisticated and subtle must be the sales presentation. If you're selling perfume to ladies, your advertising and sales approach must be very low-key and gentle. Perfume is a delicate subject used delicately; it is only sold when the salesperson can structure the appeal in such a way that it connects with deep inner needs for beauty and self-realization.

The fifth part of the law of need says that the obvious need is often not the real need upon which the product will be purchased. Never assume that you know the need. Each customer is different. The need that caused one customer to buy may not be the same for another. If you structure your appeal to the wrong need, you'll be unsuccessful in the sales process. Again, the best salespeople are very sensitive and attentive to their customers. They don't even begin to attempt to sell until they're absolutely clear what the customer is really interested in buying.

The Law of Problems

The fourth law of selling is the *law of problems*: every product or service can be viewed as the solution to a problem, the fulfillment of a need, or the resolution of an uncertainty. As a salesperson, you are basically a professional problem solver. People get from where they are to where they want to go by means of your product or service.

Every product or service can be viewed as the solution to a problem.

The first part of the law of problems says that customers buy solutions, not products or services. A businessperson, for example, is interested in increasing productivity or sales, decreasing costs, and increasing bottom-line profits. The businessperson doesn't care whether you're selling mainframe computers or hula hoops. They are interested in their problem and possible solutions to it, not your product or service or your desire to sell it.

When you begin to perceive yourself as a professional problem solver rather than as a salesperson, your success with your customers will go up dramatically.

The second part of the law of problems says that the more pressing the problem or need, the less price-sensitive the customer will be and the easier the sale. If a customer really needs a product or service, their concern about price and timing will diminish. A really hungry person will pay a lot to eat. Your job in the sales conversation is to increase the level of the customer's desire for the benefits and enjoyment of your product or service to the point where the price is not a major obstacle to proceeding.

The Law of Persuasion

The fifth law of selling is the *law of persuasion*, which says that the process of selling is convincing the customer that they will be better off with the product than they would be with the money necessary to buy the product.

You're asking the customer to engage in a trade. You're telling the customer that if they give you their money, the product or service that you'll supply will be of greater value to them than either the money or anything else they could buy with that same amount of money at the same time.

Remember the law of the excluded alternative: every choice implies a rejection. When you ask a customer to buy from you and exchange some of their limited amount of money, you're asking them to forgo all other pleasures and satisfactions that are available with the same amount of money, and this is a big question.

The first part of the law of persuasion is that the customer always acts to satisfy the greatest number of unmet needs in the best way at the lowest possible price. A major part of your job is to demonstrate that the customer will get more of what they want faster by purchasing your product or service than if they either kept the money or bought something else.

The second part of this law of persuasion says proof that others similar to the customer have already purchased the product builds credibility, lowers resistance, and increases sales. Every piece of information that shows the customer that other people similar to them have already wrestled with this buying decision, decided to go ahead, and have been happy as a result moves you closer to making the sale.

The third part of the law of persuasion says half-jokingly that salespeople who don't use testimonials have skinny kids. Testimonial letters, photos of happy customers using and enjoying your product or service, or lists of satisfied customers are extraordinarily powerful influence factors. Take full advantage of testimonials and acquire them from every source possible and every way you possibly can. They can make your sales work much easier. All top salespeople get where they are by using testimonials tied directly into the customer they're talking with and the product or services that they're selling.

The Law of Risk

The sixth law of selling is the *law of risk*, which says that risk is inherent in any investment of time, money, or emotion. Risk is an inescapable fact of life, and we always act in every way possible to reduce risk. This is the essence of the insurance industry. Insurance is simply a way of pooling risks by taking premiums from a large number of people in order to cover the losses that will be suffered by a small number of them. Insuring yourself properly can give you tremendous inner peace from the reduction of risk.

The first part of this law of risk says that you are successful in sales to the degree to which you can position yourself as the low-risk provider of your product or service. This is one of the most important concepts in selling, and you need to build it into all of your sales efforts. Many sales fail to materialize because the customer doesn't feel that they'll be safe in the use, enjoyment, or follow-up service and maintenance of the product. So you must build this idea of low risk into every sales presentation.

The second part of the law of risk says that the primary psychological obstacle to buying is the fear of failure: the fear of making a mistake in a purchasing decision. The fear of failure is one of the most powerful of all inhibitors of human action. The fear of failure in buying is rooted in previous experiences. Perhaps the customer bought a product or service that didn't work, or one that ended up costing too much. Since everyone has had bad buying experiences, everyone is conditioned to be cautious and fearful about having those experiences again. This fear of failure is a major psychological block that you must overcome before a purchase decision can be made.

The primary psychological obstacle to buying is the fear of failure.

The third part of this law says that everything you do in a sales interview either raises or lowers the prospect's perception of risk and fear of failure. Because you're asking a person to part with their money and risk their ego in a sales situation, the purchasing decision is charged with emotion. Everything about you is either adding to or detracting from the perception of risk and uncertainty on the customer's part.

In a sales situation, especially a larger sale, nothing is neutral. Everything counts. Everything that you do is either moving you toward the sale or moving you away from it. Never allow yourself the luxury of saying, "Oh, that doesn't matter." Everything matters. Everything counts. Everything is either adding or taking away. Your job is to make sure that everything you do or say is helpful in some way in lowering the perception of risk and raising the perception of security.

The Law of Trust

The seventh law of selling is the *law of trust*. One of the most important of all laws in selling, it says that the trust bond between the salesperson and the customer is the foundation of a successful sale. The higher the level of trust between you and your prospective customer, the lower will be the fear of failure and the perception of risk.

The first part of this law says that you build trust in a sales relationship by asking questions aimed at the customer's real needs that your product or service can satisfy. Many salespeople don't realize that an endless series of questions aimed at the customer's life and situation may be of interest temporarily but don't build the level of trust. Only when you ask penetrating questions aimed at the real needs of the customer that your product or service can solve will the customer warm to you and begin to believe in you.

The second part of the law of trust says that successful salespeople listen twice as much as they talk. They practice what is called the 70/30 rule. They listen 70 percent or more of the time, and they talk 30 percent or less. It's been said often that you have two ears and one mouth, and in a sales conversation, you should use them in that proportion. The best salespeople are superb listeners. Many of them are introverts and not particularly gregarious or outgoing. They're also extremely effective.

The third part of the law of trust says that no one ever listened themselves out of a sale. In many cases, if you listen patiently and intently enough—if you listen as though nothing else in the world were more important than the words of the customer at that moment—you'll listen yourself into more sales than you can imagine.

The fourth part of this law, which is as important as anything that you'll ever learn in selling, is that listening builds trust. There's no better or faster way to build trust between two people than for one to listen to the other. This is true in all relationships. You like the people best who listen to you the most attentively when you talk about something that's important to you. Customers are the same.

The Law of Relationships

The eighth law of selling is the *law of relationships*. Applied to sales, it says that success in selling is determined by the ability of the salesperson to form a quality relationship with the customer. In his book *The Marketing Imagination*, the late Theodore Levitt of the Harvard Business School explains how marketing and selling have changed in recent years: today, because of risk, uncertainty, and the variety of options available to the customer, the relationship is central in selling.

The first part of this law says that the customer wants a relationship first. Before a customer will seriously consider a complex offer of any kind, they want to be sure that they can rely upon the salesperson and the company to fulfill their commitments after the money has changed hands.

The second part of this law says that in complex sales, the relationship continues after the sale: Before buying a product or service, the customer is largely independent of the salesperson and the company; the customer doesn't need them in any way. However, once a buying decision has been made, the customer becomes dependent upon the warranties and assurances given by the company for the satisfactory use and enjoyment of the product. Because the relationship continues after the sale and often lasts as long as the customer uses the product or service, a purchase decision entails a decision to enter into a long-term relationship with the salesperson and the organization.

The third part of this law says that the relationship is more important than the product or service. Customers largely view products or services as commodities available from several sources. Because of this, the customer has to decide among competing suppliers, and the decision is almost invariably made on the basis of which salesperson and company the customer feels most comfortable forming a business relationship with.

The relationship is more important than the product or service.

Because relationships are so important in selling, the salesperson should clearly state that their philosophy and the philosophy of the company is to enter into a long-term relationship and maintain that relationship throughout the period of time that the customer will be using the product or service.

The most successful salespeople and the most successful companies establish long-term relationships with good customers. They make every effort to maintain the quality of that relationship through care, attentiveness, sensitivity, dependability, and fast follow-up to complaints and requests, plus excellent service and maintenance.

The Law of Friendship

The ninth law of selling is the *law of friendship*. This is often called the friendship factor, and it says that a person will not buy from you until they are convinced that you are their friend and acting in their best interests.

All successful business relationships are built on friendships between the parties. Good salespeople are excellent friend makers. Wherever they go, they have an easy ability to turn strangers into friends. They are relaxed, likable, and interested in others. Other people like them, and in liking them, want to do business with them. We always prefer to do business with the people we like, and we're psychologically constructed in such a way that we cannot and will not buy from people that we don't like, even if we want the product or service. The more business friendships you have, the more successful you'll be and the more money you'll earn by selling.

The Law of Positioning

The tenth law is the *law of positioning*, which says that the customer's perception of you and your company is their reality and determines their buying behavior.

In their excellent book *Positioning: The Battle for Your Mind*, authors Al Ries and Jack Trout point out that every product or service either has or must gain a position in the mind of the customer for that customer to be able to make any buying decision on it. With proper positioning, your product or service can be seen by the customer as the generic product, next to which others are merely substitutes or duplicates. Some examples of excellent positioning are Coca-Cola, Kleenex, and Xerox. In each case, these have become names for both the company and the product, but they're considered by most customers to be the product itself.

The first part of the law of positioning says that every element of dress, product, packaging, printing, and promotion creates a perception of some kind.

The second part says that top salespeople position themselves as the preferred suppliers of their products and services. In many cases, the customer will pay substantially more for the identical product or service simply because it is you who are selling it and backing it up. Your position in the customer's mind can be so strong that no other competitor can get to the customer and replace you.

The Law of Perspective

The eleventh law of selling is the *law of perspective*: the way you are viewed by your customers determines your income. How you are known, thought about, and talked about by your customers when you're not there largely determines your level of income and success in selling.

The first part of this law says that when you're viewed by the customer as working for him or her, you'll be in the top 10 percent of your field. Many thousands of customers who buy from the top salespeople have been extensively interviewed about their buying habits and their reasons for selecting one salesperson over another. The most common reason is that they feel that the salesperson really works for them rather than for the company. The customers feel that the salesperson cares more about their needs than about making a sale or satisfying the demands of the company that pays their salary.

A good question for you to ask continually is, how would it be useful for me to be viewed by my customers? If you were a fly on the wall and one of your customers were telling one of your prospects about you, what would you want the customer to say? Whatever it is, be sure that everything that you do in your interaction with each customer leaves them mentally prepared to say those things about you when you're not present.

A good question to ask is, how would it be useful for me to be viewed by my customers?

The second part of this law says that top money earners in sales are viewed as consultants, helpers, counselors, and advisors, but not as salespeople, by their customers. Another finding of this research says that customers looked upon the people that they bought from as dedicated to helping them solve their problems or achieve their goals.

The Law of Preparation

Twelfth is the *law of preparation*, which both follows from and precedes everything that I've discussed up to now about successful selling. This law says that the best salespeople prepare thoroughly before every call. This is so simple that it's often overlooked. The hallmark of the true professional, however, is thorough and exhaustive preparation over and over again before every competition.

The best salespeople are those who work on their presentations, their product knowledge, and their materials repeatedly throughout their sales careers and prior to every new sales contact. You can't imagine a top athlete who didn't train continually before every competition. In fact, the period of training for an athlete consumes far more time than the actual competition. In every field of endeavor, the most thoroughly trained and dedicated professionals rise to the top.

The first part of the law of preparation says that the salesperson with the best knowledge of the customer's real situation will be most likely to make the sale. The more time you take to thoroughly understand your prospective customer and their situation, the more likely you are to be in a position to sell at the critical moment.

The second part of the law of preparation says that sales professionals plan their questions in advance. There's a direct relationship between the quality of the problem-focused questions that you ask a customer and the likelihood of a sale. The only way to ensure that your questions are penetrating and exact is by writing them out word for word in advance.

Take Ben Feldman, a salesman for the New York Life Insurance Company. As early as 1979, Feldman had sold more life insurance than anyone in history. He sold life insurance policies with a total face value of about $1.5 billion for New York Life from 1942 to his death in 1993. He was written up in *The Guinness Book of Records* as the top salesman of all time. Feldman used to spend two hours every single night reviewing and rehearsing his materials so that he would be sharp and well prepared the next day. In his famous book *Feldman Method*, author Andrew Thomson explains that Ben Feldman's success was largely due to his ability to ask the right questions at the right time. He found that a properly worded question could turn a neutral or negative prospect into an interested customer, sometimes in just a few seconds.

The third part of this law preparation says that the salesperson with the best notes and the best preparation wins. Think your objectives through in advance of meeting the client. Write down and itemize exactly what you hope to accomplish on each visit. After the call, take careful notes and write down everything on the same sheet. Never rely on your memory. There's a Chinese saying: "The palest ink is stronger than the most powerful memory." Prior to every sales call, no matter how many times you may have visited the same customer, take a few minutes to review their file, their situation, and your own notes on what's taken place in the past. The top salespeople prepare exhaustively prior to selling, prior to their presentations, and prior to closing. They think everything through in advance and leave nothing to chance. The details make the difference.

The Law of Perverse Motivation

Finally, the thirteenth law of selling is the *law of perverse motivation*. This law says that everyone likes to buy, but no one likes to be sold. People don't like to feel that they're the recipients or the victims of a sales presentation. Most customers are very independent in their minds, and they don't like thinking they are being manipulated or pressured or coerced. They like to feel as though they're making up their own minds based on good information that's been presented to them.

The first part of the law of perverse motivation says that the best salesperson is perceived as one who helps the prospect get what he or she wants and needs.

The second part of the law of perverse motivation says that top salespeople are teachers who show their customers how products work to satisfy their needs. If ever your customer feels even for a moment that you're trying to sell them into buying something, they'll instantly resist. Since selling is something that you do *to* a person rather than *for* a person, and since the most important part of selling is the quality of the trust bond that exists between you and the customer, you can't afford to do anything that threatens it.

Finally, remember that all things are possible to the salesperson who knows what they're doing, believes in what they're doing, and loves what they're doing. If you are selling the right product or service with the right organization to the right people, your future can be unlimited.

The Laws of Sales

The law of sales. Nothing happens until a sale takes place.

The law of ambition. How high you rise is largely determined by how high you want to climb.

The law of need. Every decision to purchase a product or service is an attempt to satisfy a need or relieve a dissatisfaction.

The law of problems. Every product or service can be viewed as the solution to a problem, the fulfillment of a need, or the resolution of an uncertainty.

The law of persuasion. The process of selling is convincing the customer that they will be better off with the product than they would be with the money necessary to buy the product.

The law of risk. Risk is inherent in any investment of time, money, or emotion.

The law of trust. The trust bond between the salesperson and the customer is the foundation of a successful sale.

The law of relationships. Success in selling is determined by the ability of the salesperson to form a quality relationship with the customer.

The law of friendship. A person will not buy from you until they are convinced that you are their friend and acting in their best interests.

The law of positioning. The customer's perception of you and your company is their reality and determines their buying behavior.

The law of perspective. The way you are viewed by your customers determines your income.

The law of preparation. The best salespeople prepare thoroughly before every call.

The law of perverse motivation. Everyone likes to buy, but no one likes to be sold.

ten

The Laws of Business

Most of your possibilities for achievement will come by owning or working for private business organizations. President Calvin Coolidge once said that the business of America is business. According to the Small Business Administration, there were 33.2 million American businesses in 2023, and on average, 4.4 million businesses are started each year. They run the entire gamut from the smallest sole proprietorship working off a kitchen table to the largest corporate organization employing hundreds of thousands of people.

Our business system is very much a part of our way of life, and your ability to understand how it works can help you to be far more successful than people who never take the time to learn. The rate of change in businesses is accelerating. It's the one inevitable fact of modern business life.

This turbulence extends to the millions of smaller companies. Data from the Bureau of Labor Statistics indicate that 20 percent of new businesses fail during the first two years of being open; 45 percent fail during the first five years; and 65 percent fail during the first ten years. Only 25 percent of new businesses make it to fifteen years or more. Moreover, many new companies succeed and many larger companies grow at tremendous rates despite their size.

There are opportunities everywhere to make a significant contribution to your organization and thereby put your life and your career onto the fast track. In this chapter, you'll learn some of the laws and principles at work in business and how you can use them to your best advantage.

My business career began when I started selling soap for the local YMCA at the age of ten. From there, I went on to selling newspapers, lawn mowing services, and Christmas trees, and working in a department store. I went on to selling office supplies, real estate investment, automobiles, advertising, and training and consulting. I have worked in, sold, or managed small and large organizations over the course of decades, and I've seen both exciting successes and spectacular failures. By applying some of the laws and principles below, I managed and operated tens of millions of dollars' worth of companies, products, and projects. My final job in the private sector before turning to managing my own business full-time was as a chief operating officer of a $265 million company with $75 million in annual sales.

I've seen many kinds of businesses, from the most well thought out to the most ridiculous. I've worked with virtually every kind of businessperson, from the most accomplished and skillful to the most foolish and self-deluded. I've read hundreds of books and thousands of articles on various aspects of business and business management, and I still believe that I'm only scratching the surface.

Nonetheless, I've picked up a few pointers that have been instrumental in enabling me to build successful businesses of my own and help many of my clients dramatically improve their rates of growth, market shares, and profitability. There are fourteen laws that apply specifically to any business.

The Law of Purpose

First is the *law of purpose* as it applies to business, which says that the purpose of a business is to create and keep a customer. Many people think that the purpose of a business is to make a profit. Although that may be the purpose of the individual who starts or invests in the business, a business is really a separate entity, and it has a purpose of its own. In fact, a good way to assess the reason for a business's existence is to imagine that the owners had to appear in front of a tribunal each year and make a case to justify getting permission for it to carry on. You'll see immediately that making a profit in itself wouldn't cut any ice in terms of the business making sufficient contributions to justify its continued operation.

The purpose of a business is to create and keep a customer.

The first part of the law of purpose says that profits are a measure of how well a company is fulfilling its purpose. Since the purpose of a business is to create and keep a customer, how well the organization and everyone in it contribute toward that purpose will determine the company's profits.

You can tell that customer creation is the purpose of a business by observing that the time and attention of the most important people in a successful company are usually focused on its customers. Financial results are simply used as a measure of how well the primary purpose is being achieved.

The second part of the law of purpose in business says that profits are a cost of doing business: the cost of the future. Many people are confused about profit. Some consider profit to be a mark of greed; many nations have been ruined by confusion over this point. Profits are good. They that pay for everything: wages and salaries, taxes, investment in new products and processes, research and development, and all the many constructive things that a company can do when it's serving its customers well.

The opposite of profit is loss. Where there is loss, there are layoffs, reductions in economic activity, and often the collapse of the business. Where there are losses in businesses, there's no future for the people who work there. Anyone who is opposed to profit is simultaneously, whether they know it or not, opposed to the future of all the people who depend upon that business for their livelihoods. These people can't have a future where no profit exists. Wherever a society has lots of profitable companies, it has lots of well-paying jobs and great opportunities for the future. In the United States, as of December 2023, the average percentage of corporate profits was 10.96, as opposed to a long-term average of 7.18 percent.

On the other hand, the most impoverished and depressed countries in the world are those where the profit motive has been denigrated to the point where nobody makes much of anything. In those countries, opportunities for the average person are almost nonexistent.

The Law of Organization

The second law of business is the *law of organization*, which says that a business organization is merely a group of people brought together for the common purpose of creating and keeping customers. A business organization begins to form when the jobs associated with serving customers become too great for a single person. New jobs are then created and new activities are engaged in. This growth process continues as long as the increase in employees increases the number of customers that are satisfied profitably by that organization.

The Law of Customer Satisfaction

The third law of business is the *law of customer satisfaction*, which says that the customer is always right. The best companies in America are built on this philosophy. As Tom Peters said in his book *In Search of Excellence*, the best companies and the best people in those companies are obsessed with customer service. Worldwide, the most successful companies are those for whom the customer is king or queen and customer satisfaction is the driving force of all their activities.

The first comment on the law of customer satisfaction says that all customer satisfaction comes from *people*. You can't satisfy people with machines or pieces of paper. People are intensely emotional; therefore they can only be pleased in their buying activities when dealing with other people.

For this reason, the most successful companies have very clear customer policies, and everyone within those organizations is committed to treating the customers well. For example, the Walt Disney Corporation hires thousands of college students to work at the Disney theme parks in the summertime. These students are hired in the middle of May and trained in their functions for four to six weeks. They then work for approximately eight weeks of the summer season, when children are out of school. When the Disney people are asked why the students receive such rigorous training for four to six solid weeks to work for only eight weeks before going back to school, their reply reveals a lot about the Disney philosophy toward customers. The Disney managers explain that the students are drilled in their jobs to the point where they can do them virtually without thinking. The aim is to allow the students to pay more attention to their guests (as they call the visitors). Because the students have memorized their jobs completely, they are more conscious of the small things they can do to make people happy.

The second comment on the law of customer satisfaction is that the best companies invariably have the best people. The best companies learned a long time ago that 95 percent of their success will be determined by the people they select. If the wrong person is hired, they can cause a great deal of harm before they're encouraged to go somewhere else. The best companies therefore take a long time to hire people, and they're very careful in both interviewing and checking references. As you evolve into management, you learn that your biggest successes will come from having chosen the right people for the key positions under you.

The third comment on the law of customer satisfaction is that the key role of management is to achieve the maximum return on investment in human resources by satisfying customers. With regard to any job, managers have two choices: they can do the job themselves or they can get someone else to do it. The job of the manager is to act as a multiplier and get things done through others rather than to do it himself or herself.

One final observation on customer satisfaction: the staff will always treat the customers the way management treats them. Whenever you're treated especially well by people in any store or restaurant, you know that that place has a good manager. Whenever you're treated poorly for any reason, you know that the person you are dealing with is usually attempting to get back at a manager who, they feel, is treating them badly.

**The staff will always treat the customers
the way management treats them.**

The Law of the Customer

The fourth law of business is the *law of the customer*: the customer always acts to satisfy his or her interests by seeking the very most at the very lowest possible price. Customers are economical in that they seek to maximize their resources and minimize their outlays. Customers follow the law of expediency in that they attempt to get the things they want the fastest and easiest way possible, right now, with no concern for secondary or long-term consequences.

These are all facts of business life; they're not problems. In business, you're continually faced with both facts and problems. Facts are inevitable and unavoidable parts of life: things that you accept and work around. They're like immovable objects.

A problem, on the other hand, is something that you can solve using your intelligence and imagination. It's very important in business that you separate facts from problems and avoid becoming upset over something about which you can do nothing. Before you become concerned about something that has or has not happened, ask yourself, is this a problem or is this a fact?

The first part of the law of the customer says that customers are both demanding and ruthless. They'll highly reward those companies that serve them best and allow those companies that serve them poorly to fail. It isn't that customers don't care about a particular business; it's just that customers care about themselves and their own satisfactions more than they care about the success or failure of an enterprise.

Whenever you see a business fail, you see an entity whose owners were either unable or unwilling to adjust their actions to serve enough customers at prices that allow the company to carry on. The customers just silently walked away, told their friends, and never came back.

The second part of the law of the customer says that customers always behave rationally in pursuing the path of least resistance to satisfy their most pressing needs. From the customers' point of view, every action makes perfect sense. All their behavior is aimed at achieving greater personal satisfaction and improving their position.

The customer is very smart and always knows what is in their best interests. The customer's decision is always rational. The customer is always right. When you go into business, you put your entire financial future at the mercy of satisfying the customer every single day. From the moment you open your doors, the customer determines what you will sell, how much of it you will sell, at what price you will sell it, and how much money you will make. It's only by catering to the customer's whims and fancies that you'll be able to survive and grow in business.

The third part of this law says that proper business planning always begins with the customer as the central focus of attention and discussion. People within companies have a dangerous tendency to lose touch with the real thoughts, feelings, and needs of their customers. People in these companies tend to talk to themselves too much and, what's worse, they listen to each other and become divorced from reality. If you're in business and if what you do affects the customer, you should mentally erect a statue of the customer and place it in the middle of the table when you discuss what you are going to do with your products or services. Always ask yourself, if the customer were sitting here listening to us, what would the customer be thinking? What would the customer say? Would the customer approve or disapprove of what we're planning to do?

The customer is very important. Some people within organizations have the mistaken idea that they have no customers because they don't interact with the person who buys the company's product or service. This can be a fatal mistake. The fact is that everyone has a customer; in fact, you may have several customers. Your primary customer is the person who determines your success in your job. By this definition, unless you're the boss, your number one customer is your boss: whether or not you satisfy your boss determines how far and how fast you move ahead. If you're a manager and you have people working under you, your staff are your customers. It's how you satisfy them that will determine how they satisfy the people who must use what your department produces. If you work in accounting or administration, your customers are the people who must use what you produce, such as financial statements, computer printouts, or other information. Everyone has a customer. Everyone is in the business of customer satisfaction. Everyone's level of success is determined by how well they satisfy the most important customers they have.

The Law of Quality

The fifth law of business is the *law of quality*, which states that the customer demands the very highest quality for the very lowest price. This seems simple enough, except that many companies try to violate this law on their way to the bankruptcy courts. The customer is very smart. The customer will always act to satisfy the greatest number of possible needs in any particular buying decision. Only companies that cater to the customer's incessant need for ever higher levels of quality are successful in the marketplace. For example, in 1989, both the Toyota Lexus and the Nissan Infiniti were released for sale in the United States. Both companies advertised these cars as the cars of the future with every luxury feature of the more expensive European cars, but at prices that were $10,000, $20,000, or even $30,000 cheaper. Both companies committed themselves to building the finest quality automobiles in their class in America.

In 1991, the J.D. Power survey came out with results of customer satisfaction for all 557 models of automobile sold in the United States. According to their rankings, the Lexus and the Infiniti were tied for first place in quality. Even before these results came out, because of the companies' commitment to quality, the sales of these cars had taken off into the hundreds of millions of dollars.

The first part of the law of quality says that quality is what the customer says it is and is willing to pay for. Only the customer can define quality. Sometimes the customer can't even define it clearly, but they will vote for quality by the way they spend their dollars.

In his book *Quality without Tears: The Art of Hassle-Free Management*, Philip B. Crosby wrote that quality is fairly easy to define: the quality of a product can be measured by the percentage of the time it does what it is sold to do and continues to do it. In other words, you can measure the quality of a watch by how long it continues to tell perfect time. If it does so 100 percent of the time for the indefinite future, then it has a 100 percent quality rating. If you buy a car, the quality rating of that car is how long it continues to give you trouble-free service without needing repairs or maintenance, aside from those specified at the time of purchase. If the car runs trouble-free for 100 percent of the time, then it has a 100 percent quality rating. Unfortunately, it's not uncommon for fully 25 percent of products manufactured in some plants to have to be reworked and rebuilt at the factory because of quality defects.

The quality of a product can be measured by the percentage of the time it does what it is sold to do and continues to do it.

In another book, *Quality Is Free*, Crosby points out that manufacturing a high-quality item without defects saves money and boosts profit, both in the short term and the long term. In the short term, quality creates customers, and in the long term, quality keeps customers.

The second part of this law says that quality refers both to the product or service and to the way that it is sold, delivered, and maintained. *Quality* actually refers to all of the activities associated with the purchase, ownership, and possession of the item. For example, prices in a quality restaurant are not based only on the fact that good food is served on the plate. A high-class restaurant, one that commands above average prices and can earn above average profits, serves the food in an atmosphere of comfort and enjoyment that people are willing to pay more for.

Even a simple product can be sold and served with cheerfulness and courtesy, thereby increasing its perceived value. The customer defines the total experience: both product and service are part of the impression of quality.

The third part of the law of quality is that companies are financially successful in direct proportion to their quality ranking as customers perceive it. If a market researcher were to go into the marketplace and conduct an honest, objective survey amongst customers, it could come up with a ranking for your company in terms of how it compares to your competitors. For example, suppose there are ten companies doing the same thing in the same market area. A survey could indicate which of these companies is perceived to be number one in that marketplace. The survey could also determine which companies would rank as number two, number three, and so on. The evidence shows that the companies that are perceived to be the highest-quality companies in any marketplace are also the most profitable ones in that marketplace.

This is because of the deep human need for security. Whenever a person has to choose between a higher-priced product and a lower-priced product, if they can possibly afford it, they will choose the higher-priced product, because a higher price is associated with greater quality. The perception of better quality reduces the feeling of uncertainty or risk in making the buying decision. That's why it's said, if you can afford to buy quality, you can't afford *not* to.

There's almost always a direct relationship between the amount that you pay and the quality of the product or service. You seldom get good quality at a low price. You never get something for nothing. You usually get what you pay for. In a competitive society, you can be reasonably sure that the higher price will assure you a higher level of quality and a lower level of risk. It gives customers greater security to purchase a high-priced, high-quality product than if they saved a little money and bought a lower-quality item. There's a saying by the British art critic John Ruskin: "The bitterness of poor quality is remembered long after the pleasure of low price has been forgotten."

Wherever you are in the quality rankings (and almost everyone knows where they are, even without surveys), you must commit yourself and your company to the number-one position.

You must commit to becoming the very best in your chosen field. Aim for quality leadership. Not only will it animate and excite everybody in the organization to be committed to such a worthwhile goal, but it will also be reflected in your profits. The highest-quality company is the one that earns the greatest profits and represents the greatest opportunities for the future. The most successful companies continually innovate and bring out new products and new services, even when business is slow.

The Law of Obsolescence

The sixth law of business is the *law of obsolescence*: whatever is, is already becoming obsolete. Products, services, advertisements, marketing strategies, and every other plan or policy in an organization are becoming obsolete with rapid speed. As a result, you and your company must be fast on your feet and prepared to accept continual change as an unavoidable fact of life.

The first part of the law of obsolescence says that tomorrow will be different from today. The most frustrated people in business are those who are trying to hold back the tide by failing to adapt or by adapting too slowly to the competitive onslaught that's taking place all around them.

The second part of this law says that continuous innovation and improvement are essential to survival. They are not luxuries to be engaged in only when there's sufficient time and money. Every company must have top-quality people who are absolutely dedicated full-time to developing the products and services of tomorrow. If a company doesn't do this, it will end up having no tomorrow. It'll be bypassed by competitors who are eager to take the business. There's a direct relationship between the quantity of new ideas the company comes up with and its ultimate financial success. So innovate, innovate, innovate.

The third part of the law of obsolescence says that the best way to predict the future is to create it. Be like Walt Disney: when he was asked if he was worried about people stealing his ideas, he replied, "We'll come up with new ideas faster than anyone can possibly steal them."

This should be your philosophy as well. You should always have more ideas for good products and services to bring to the market than you possibly have resources to develop. You should always be forced to select among a variety of possibilities, to choose the ones that have the greatest market potential at that moment.

The Law of Innovation

The seventh law of business is the *law of innovation*, which is closely tied to the law of obsolescence. It states that all business breakthroughs come from innovation, from offering something better, cheaper, faster, newer, or more efficiently in the current marketplace.

A person working for a company can often see a need for a product or service that can revolutionize both the company and that individual's life. For example, a scientist at 3M Corporation in Minnesota who sang in the local church choir was having a tough time getting a bookmark to stick in the pages of his hymn book. He experimented with a variety of glues looking for an adhesive that would enable a piece of paper to stick on and come off several times without leaving a mark or losing its stickiness. He came up with Post-its, creating the entire market for stick-on notes. As of 2019, 3M still dominated the $2.19 billion sticky notes market, at 77.4

percent. And the gentleman who came up with the idea became a wealthy man.

In Peter Drucker's marvelous book *Innovation and Entrepreneurship*, he talks about the seven major sources of innovation, and he gives a variety of ideas on how to make innovation a way of life, both for yourself and for your corporation. All you need is one good idea, either within your company or on your own, to start you on the high road to great business success.

The Law of Critical Success Factors

The eighth law of business is the *law of critical success factors*. It's based on research summarized in a *Harvard Business Review* article from 1982. This law says that every business has approximately five to seven critical success factors, the performance of which determine the success or failure of the enterprise. Critical success factors are like the vital functions of the body, such as heart rate, respiratory rate, and blood pressure. They indicate life and vitality, and the absence of any one of them, even for a few moments, signals the death of the organism.

Companies also have critical success factors, many of which they have in common and some of which are individual to each organization. Some of the most common critical success factors could be leadership, product quality, marketing and sales, manufacturing, distribution, finance, and accounting. Excellent performance is necessary in every one of these areas for a company to enjoy excellent results. Poor performance or nonperformance in any area can threaten the life of the enterprise. For example, according Dunn and Bradstreet, 46 percent of business failures in the United States are triggered by a drop-off in sales and marketing and sales revenue. This, then, is a critical success factor or vital function of the business.

The first part of this law says that every individual also has critical success factors, the performance of which determines his or her success. Each person, including yourself, has a set of core skills or core competencies that they use like tools to do their job. A weakness or failure in any one of a person's core skills can render that person incapable of doing their job correctly.

For example, problem solving and decision-making are critical functions of every manager and every executive. A person who is physically ill or going through an extremely emotional period may not be capable of solving problems intelligently or making good decisions. Everyone who depends upon that person for these abilities can have their own performance curtailed. An entire department can grind slowly to a halt because of a malfunction in a critical success factor of a single person.

A single weakness in one critical success factor of selling can cause a person to sell only a small part of which they're capable. In many companies, the sales force has been poorly trained or not trained at all, and the senior management is beside themselves, wondering why they're not getting the sales they need to survive. Sometimes a little sales training can double or even triple the average sales of an organization.

To determine your critical success factors, you can ask yourself two sets of questions. You should repeat them every day as long as you are in the world of work. The first of these sets of questions is, "Why am I on the payroll? What have I been hired to accomplish? What results am I responsible for?" The second set is, "What can I and only I do that, if done well, will make a real difference to my company? What is the one thing that I and only I can do that can really help my company, that can make an extraordinary difference in my results?"

These two questions—"why am I on the payroll?" and "what can I and only I do that, being done well, will make a real difference?"—should be asked of every single person in the organization on a regular basis so that everyone is absolutely clear about the answers. This is the one way to ensure that each person is performing at the necessary levels in their critical success factors.

The Law of the Market

The ninth law of business is the *law of the market*. This states that the market is where buyers and sellers of products and services meet to set prices and determine the allocations of money, labor, natural resources, and all other factors of production.

Now the market is a fictitious place, but it represents all of the millions of buying and selling decisions that take place every day at every level of society and in every area of private and public enterprise. The synthesis of all these decisions by millions of customers, acting out the law of expediency, determines the prices of virtually everything that's not government-controlled in our society.

The first part of the law of the market says that according to the efficient market thesis, in a free market, resources will be allocated with complete efficiency, and prices will accurately reflect supply and demand at that moment.

In a free market, resources will be allocated with complete efficiency, and prices will accurately reflect supply and demand at that moment.

This efficient market thesis is usually applied to the stock market. It says that all stock prices at the close of each day will accurately reflect all the information that is known about the present and future prospects of the company, represented by the shares. This thesis also suggests that knowledge of changing prices will spread rapidly to the people whose economic interests might be affected.

The second part of the law of the market says that the free market is the most efficient way for millions of people to have their needs met at the lowest possible cost. The free market exists automatically in the absence of government controls on wages, prices, or economic activities. The freer the market, the more vibrant the economy and the greater amount of wealth and opportunity that's created.

Every attempt to interfere with the freedom of the marketplace is done for a reason that sounds good, but the real reason is that it benefits special interests and penalizes the customers by forcing them to pay more for a product or service than they would have if the market was free. To put it another way, interference in the marketplace never reduces prices for anyone on any product or service at any time.

The Law of Specialization

The tenth law of business is the *law of specialization*, which is closely tied to the law of the market. It says that to succeed in a competitive marketplace, a product or service must be both specialized and excellent at satisfying a clearly defined need of the customer. It must be clear what the product is designed to do and whom the product is designed to do it for.

The law of specialization also says that companies fail when they no longer specialize or serve a sufficient number of customers in a cost-efficient way.

Specialization is the starting point of successful marketing. It must be made clear what you are offering and for whom.

The Law of Differentiation

The eleventh law of business is the *law of differentiation*, which states that in order to succeed in a marketplace, a product must have an area of uniqueness that makes it stand out from its competitors in some way. It cannot be a me-too product. It has to have special strengths or qualities that make it different and better than any of the other products or services that can be used as a substitute for it.

The first part of the law of differentiation says that the determination of a unique selling proposition is the beginning of all successful advertising and sales. A company should be able to summarize what makes its product or service unique and different in twenty-five words or less. For many years, Ivory soap was famous for its simple advertisement, which said "99 and 44/100 percent pure." Ivory followed up with the slogan: "It floats!" When it was competing against large American cars, Volkswagen came up with an advertising line emphasizing its unique selling proposition: "Volkswagen. It makes your house look bigger."

The best marketing, advertising, and selling campaigns are built around a unique selling proposition that can be communicated in a meaningful way to the prospective customer.

The second part of the law of differentiation says that to survive and thrive in the marketplace, a product or service must have a competitive advantage, something that makes it superior to competing products and services.

Determining the competitive advantage of the product or service is perhaps the most important single marketing decision made by a company or organization. Whether it's a national newspaper like *USA Today* or a candidate for political office, the advertisers must create a meaningful competitive advantage that gives the prospective customer a good reason to buy that product rather than something else.

Jack Welch, the late CEO of General Electric, said that his philosophy was to be either number one or number two in every market area in which General Electric competed. He went on to say, "If you don't have competitive advantage, don't compete."

So what is your competitive advantage? In what way or ways is your product or service superior to that of your competitors? If you don't have a competitive advantage, what could it be? What should it be? Without a competitive advantage, the product or service is doomed in the marketplace.

The Law of Segmentation

Twelfth is the *law of segmentation*: which says that companies must target specific customer groups or market segments if they are to achieve significant sales. We are rapidly reaching the end of the mass market. Today the most successful companies are those that have been able to identify specific segments of the marketplace, for whom they design individualized products and services to satisfy special groups of needs and tastes. The Ford Mustang was so successful when it was launched in part because it was the first car that could be customized with so many different colors and accessories that almost every single Mustang was unique and different. This satisfied the individual's craving to own an automobile that stood out rather than one that was lost in the crowd.

The first part of the law of segmentation in business is that many companies fail because they're targeting the wrong market with the wrong product in the wrong way. Many companies start off targeting their advertising in sales at a particular market segment, only to find that the products are being purchased by a different market segment altogether.

Light pickups were originally designed for construction work and hauling small quantities and materials. However, they became extremely popular with young people as sports vehicles for going to the beach or the mountains.

For many years, Löwenbräu beer, a high-priced German import, tried to compete with American beers such as Budweiser and Miller. Löwenbräu tried every conceivable form of advertising but was still unable to break into markets that were tied up by the big breweries. Finally, they changed their marketing strategy and began targeting men and women with higher incomes. The first advertisement they came out with using this new strategy changed the whole history of imported beer in the United States. It simply said, "When you run out of champagne, order Löwenbräu." By positioning themselves against champagne rather than against lower-priced beer, they created a perception that imported beer was something to be drunk by people who could afford only the best.

The fate of Löwenbräu, by the way, illustrates the law of quality. In 1975, the Miller Brewing Company acquired the North American rights to Löwenbräu. Miller began brewing the beer with an Americanized recipe instead of the German version, which abided strictly by the German *Reinheitsgebot* (or "purity order"), which stipulated that beer could only contain barley, water, and hops, although Miller pretended that it was using the original German recipe. When the truth was revealed, sales of Löwenbräu plummeted. A palpable drop in quality ended any appreciable place for it in the American beer market.

The second part of the law of segmentation says that the ideal market segment contains those customers for whom the product's competitive advantage satisfies their most pressing needs.

The whole purpose of market research is to answer these questions: Who is your ideal customer? Why does the customer buy? Why does the customer refrain from buying? Why does the customer buy from your competitor? The more accurate you are about the customer you're trying to create and keep, the more focused your marketing efforts will be and the more likely it is that your company will succeed in the marketplace.

The Law of Concentration

The thirteenth law of business is the *law of concentration*: market success comes from single-mindedly concentrating on selling to those customers for whom the product's area of differentiation is the most valuable and important.

To use the examples of Lexus and Infiniti, when they were first introduced, these two cars competed in a specific market niche or segment: their marketing efforts concentrated on selling to men and women who admired Mercedes and BMW but for whom these cars were out of their price range. These were generally well-paid, upscale, college-educated, white-collar professionals. The car manufacturers knew that the further down the price curve they could go, the greater the number of potential customers who could buy their product. (Today the price ranges for all of these cars are much closer to one another.)

The first part of the law of concentration says that one of the best high-profit strategies is to dominate a specific market niche with the best product available for those customers in that niche. One example of dominating a specific market niche with a high-quality product was the A. T. Cross pen company. For a long time, Cross pens managed to position themselves in the minds of American businesspeople as the premier high-quality American business pen, with pens that ranged from black all the way up to eighteen-karat gold. For a long time, competitors such as Parker and Montblanc had great difficulty in penetrating the American luxury pen market, and to this day, Cross remains a leading company in this field.

The second part of the law of concentration says that concentration on high-profit market segments with high-profit products gives the highest return on sales, return on investment, and return on equity. The most profitable companies in America are those selling high-profit products in high-profit markets. The companies that manufacture the best, highest-quality, most expensive products invariably earn the highest possible profits on the sales of those products. The Rolex watch company is one example.

The Law of Excellence

The fourteenth law is the *law of excellence*, which says that the market always pays excellent rewards for excellent performance, excellent products, and excellent services. Moreover, the market pays average rewards for average performance and below average rewards for below average performance. The market is a just taskmaster. It is always fair. It is always equitable. It always reflects the true expressed intentions of the customers. It always rewards those who serve it with the goods and services it wants at prices it's willing to pay, and it always punishes those companies who refuse to do so by simply declining to buy their offerings.

The key to earning excellent rewards in your career is to become excellent at performing your critical success functions in satisfying your most important customers.

The keys to business success have always been the same. A thousand books have been written and countless articles have been published, but they all eventually come down to what I call the basic five:

1. The product or service must be ideally suited to the existing market and to what people want, need, and are willing to pay for. Products that are not ideally suited to the existing market must change quickly or run the risk of disappearing.

2. There must be a company-wide focus on marketing, sales, and revenue generation. The most important energies of the most talented people in the company must center on the customer and on selling more to ever larger numbers of customers. Failure to do this is the number one cause of business collapse in any economy.

3. There must be efficient internal systems of bookkeeping, accounting, inventory management, and cost control. Losing control of internal costs and internal operations is the number two reason for business failure.

4. There must be a clear sense of direction and a high level of synergy and teamwork among the managers and staff. The company should function like a well-oiled machine, with a place for everyone and everyone in their place, performing at their best.

5. The company should never stop learning, growing, innovating, and improving. The Japanese call this process *kaizen*. W. Edwards Deming, the father of quality, was convinced that continuous training and upgrading at all levels of the company is the key to achieving meaningful competitive advantage and to business success.

The American free enterprise system, where you, I, and everyone else have the freedom to enter the marketplace to attempt to serve customers with goods and services in better ways or at cheaper prices than anyone else, is the finest system ever evolved for the satisfaction of needs and the creation of opportunity. You can take your place in this system by offering a product or service that people want and are willing to pay for. By practicing these laws of business, you can build a successful company that brings you all the rewards and satisfactions you desire.

The Laws of Business

The law of purpose. The purpose of a business is to create and keep a customer.

The law of organization. A business organization is merely a group of people brought together for the common purpose of creating and keeping customers.

The law of customer satisfaction. The customer is always right.

The law of the customer. The customer always acts to satisfy his or her interests by seeking the very most at the very lowest possible price.

The law of quality. The customer demands the very highest quality for the very lowest price.

The law of obsolescence. Whatever is, is already becoming obsolete. Products, services, advertisements, marketing strategies, and every other plan or policy in an organization are becoming obsolete with rapid speed. You must be prepared to accept continual change as an unavoidable fact of life.

The law of innovation. All business breakthroughs come from innovation, from offering something better, cheaper, faster, newer, or more efficient in the current marketplace.

The law of critical success factors. Every business has approximately five to seven critical success factors, the performance of which determine the success or failure of the enterprise.

The law of the market. The market is where buyers and sellers of products and services meet to set prices and determine the allocations of money, labor, natural resources, and all other factors of production.

The law of specialization. To succeed in a competitive marketplace, a product or service must be both specialized and excellent at satisfying a clearly defined need of the customer.

The law of differentiation. To succeed in the marketplace, a product must have an area of uniqueness that makes it stand out from its competitors.

The law of segmentation. Companies must target specific customer groups or market segments if they are to achieve significant sales.

The law of concentration. Market success comes from single-mindedly concentrating on selling to those customers for whom the product's area of differentiation is the most valuable and important.

The law of excellence. The market always pays excellent rewards for excellent performance, excellent products, and excellent services.

eleven

The Laws of Luck

We live in a world governed by laws and principles, many of which we know in full and many of which we only know in part. Earlier in this book, I said that the laws of cause and effect, action and reaction, sowing and reaping, rule the world and that there are no accidents. Success and failure happen for specific reasons. There are causes for every effect, even if we don't know exactly what they are. We have to assume, on the basis of our experience and intuition, that these laws are largely true to the extent that they have high predictive value. You can largely determine what will happen in any situation by applying the laws and principles that I've discussed. When individuals and their activities are in harmony with these laws, they can be largely assured of success in whatever they attempt. However, if anyone tries to achieve anything in violation of these laws, failure is likely to follow.

This brings us to the conclusion that luck is not an accident either. It's also subject to the law of cause and effect and many other laws as well. Luck is largely predictable, and you can increase it in your life if you understand it better. You can in effect become a very lucky person.

Luck seems to be associated with almost every great success. People are always claiming to have been lucky or have been accused of being lucky when they achieve something out of the ordinary. However, when athletes win great competitions, musicians rise to the top of their fields, craftsmen build fine pieces of furniture, or doctors achieve brilliant medical successes, the word *luck* is seldom if ever used.

Why? Because we attribute these successes to visible, predictable activities, especially hard work, preparation, and full utilization of the individual's natural talents. We ascribe success in these competitive arenas to the individual's education, experience, training and application, but we seldom accuse the person of having merely been lucky.

People usually use *luck* to describe things that happen that they don't understand and can't explain. You, like everyone else, have a strong need to make sense of your life and what is going on around you. Psychologists call this a need for a sense of coherence or an understanding of how things hang together. When this sense of coherence is threatened by things that seem to happen by chance, either positive or negative, we reassert mental order and peace of mind by writing it off to luck of some kind. Once you can say, "He was just lucky" or "I just got a lucky break," it gives you a sense of comfort and security and enables you to stop thinking about how and why a particular thing happened.

Interestingly, successful people tend to both feel lucky and be lucky, and they often attribute their successes to luck. Sometimes they say this to avoid the envy attached to high achievement: they claim they were just lucky so they appear humble and ordinary in the eyes of others.

Unsuccessful people, on the other hand, attribute much of the success of others to luck rather than talent. At the same time, they blame most of their own failures on bad luck, as though in their cases the law of cause and effect had somehow been suspended, thereby making them the unfortunate and undeserving victims of chance.

Deep in their hearts, most successful people attribute their achievements to hard work far beyond the ordinary. They say things like, "The harder I work, the luckier I get." They believe that they have earned their success and that they deserve the occasional lucky break that seems to propel them forward far faster than the ordinary.

The fact is, your luck can be managed and increased by applying certain mental and physical laws. What you're about to learn about luck and success could change your future. There are twelve laws of luck, which in conjunction with the other laws you've learned in this book, can help you to accomplish more in a shorter time than perhaps you ever thought possible.

Your luck can be managed and increased by applying certain mental and physical laws.

The Law of Probability

The first law of luck is the *law of probability*. This law says that there is a mathematical probability of the occurrence of any event which can be deduced with considerable accuracy from observation, measurement, and experience.

There's an entire school of mathematics called *game theory*, which measures the probabilities of a particular event occurring out of a particular number or sequence of events. For example, when you toss a coin, it will come down heads 50 percent of the time, and it will come down tails 50 percent of the time. If you toss the coin 10 times or 1,000 times, there's still a 50/50 probability of the coin coming down heads or tails. The probabilities don't change, although they don't predict what will happen on each individual coin toss.

In the 1950s, the likelihood of dying in a plane crash in the United States was approximately one in 1 million flights. With the dramatic increases in air safety that have taken place in the last few decades, the likelihood of dying in a plane crash in the United States is now one in eleven million flights. We still can't predict which airplane will crash, but we know that the likelihood of being injured or killed in a plane crash is extremely low, almost equivalent to the likelihood of winning a state lottery or being struck by lightning.

Gambling casinos are designed on certain probabilities of the house winning at each game. Blackjack, for example, is the game that offers the greatest probabilities in favor of the gambler: about 45 percent. This means that in blackjack, the house will win 55 percent of the time. Although gambling casinos never go out of business because of losses, countless gamblers go home broke because of this small difference in probabilities.

The first part of the law of probability says that you can increase the probability of an event occurring by increasing the number of events. This is so obvious as to not even require discussion, but many people overlook it. For example, the president of Amoco Petroleum, a company with a long record of finding more gas and oil than competing petroleum companies, was once asked why his company was so much more successful than his competitors. He replied by pointing out that all companies have access to the same data and use pretty much the same geologists, geophysicists, and oil engineers, with pretty much the same abilities. Amoco was more successful than its rivals because, he said, "we drill more holes." There was no miracle. They simply increased the quantity of wells they drilled and thereby increased the quantity of proven and probable gas and oil reserves.

The second part of the law of probability says that probabilities increase with persistence. The longer you persist in a string of failures, the more likely you are to get lucky. There's a poem by John Greenleaf Whittier entitled "Don't Quit," which has the lines, "You never can tell how close you are. / It may be near when it seems so far."

The most successful people persist in the face of all adversity, long after the average person would have given up, and sure enough, by the law of probability, things start to go their way. They get their lucky break.

The third part of this law says that you are both the batter and umpire in your ball game of life. You are the batter at the plate, swinging at each pitch. In a normal baseball game, if you swing and miss three times, you'd be out. However, in your own personal ball game, you are also your own umpire, and only you can call yourself out. You can continue to swing as long and as hard as you want; you're never out until you decide to be out.

The Law of Clarity

The second law of luck is the *law of clarity*: the clearer you are about what you want and what you're willing to do to get it, the greater the probability that you'll experience luck.

It's been said that the two keys to great success are, first, being clear about what you want, and, second, being clear about the price you're going to pay to get it.

Personally, I'm a strong believer in clarity. I believe that people are happy or unhappy to the degree to which they're clear about the key issues of their lives. Most problems seem to come from lack of clarity.

The first part of this law says that intensely desired goals activate your reticular cortex and make you aware of opportunities you might have overlooked. If you decide to lose weight, you begin to see all kinds of articles and information on diet, exercise, and weight loss. If you decide to earn more money, you begin to notice all kinds of possibilities for reducing your costs and increasing your income.

The second part of the law of clarity says that the more you want something, the more alert you will be to your chance to achieve it when it comes. The law of clarity is closely aligned with intensity of desire and purpose, both of which make you much more sensitive to the chance word or remark that may help you.

For example, some years ago, a friend of mine graduated from university in a medium-sized town in one of the western states. He got the idea that if he were to go to a place such as New York, he might discover a new business opportunity that he could bring back that hadn't yet been introduced into his city. Against the advice of others, he purchased a plane ticket and flew east. During the four-hour flight, he got into a conversation with a man sitting next to him. It turned out that this man was a business development officer for a large franchise organization who had been out to his city looking for a franchisee. He'd been unsuccessful and was on his way home. The franchise turned out to be Orange Julius. When my friend asked him about his business and got the details, he became so excited that he signed the franchise agreement right there on the plane. When they got off the plane together, my friend turned around and went back home on the next return flight. As a result of that chance meeting, which took place because he was so clear about what he was looking for, he went on to rent the last space in a new shopping center and subsequently built an extremely successful business. This business generated the cash flow that financed a series of other business investments, which made him a millionaire by the time he was twenty-five. There are countless stories like this that have their roots in clarity, purpose, and desire. They all increase the incidents of luck.

The Law of Attraction

The third law of luck is the *law of attraction*, which I've already mentioned and which is very much at work in the area of luck. To repeat, it says that you inevitably attract into your life the people, ideas, circumstances, and resources that harmonize with your dominant thoughts. Because of this law, whatever you can hold in your mind on a continuing basis, you can have; the only limitations are the limitations you place on your own thinking.

The first part of the law of attraction as it applies to luck simply says that what you want wants you. When you think about something that you intensely desire, you magnetize this thought, and you begin to send out waves of mental energy that connect with resources that are in harmony with your thinking. These resources tend to be attracted to you when you're clear about what you want.

The second part of the law of attraction says that what you are moving toward is moving toward you. By the law of accelerating acceleration, when you begin to think repeatedly about something that you want, you begin almost imperceptibly to move toward it, and wherever it is, it begins to move toward you. This is one of the secrets of great riches.

The Law of Expectations

Fourth is the *law of expectations*, which I have already mentioned. With regard to luck, it says that you can increase the amount of luck in your life by continually expecting lucky things to happen.

You can increase the amount of luck in your life by continually expecting lucky things to happen.

There's something remarkable about an attitude of positive self-expectancy. It actually causes things to happen in a manner consistent with what you expect. It's called the *self-fulfilling prophecy*, and it's one of the most dependable and predictable of all mental phenomena. Lucky and successful people are always saying things like, "Don't worry; something will turn up," no matter what kind of problems they're faced with. An attitude of calmness, clarity, and self-assurance seems to create a mental climate that triggers positive events in your life.

The first part of the law of expectation says that you should look for the opportunity in every situation. You've heard it said that in Chinese the word *crisis* is written in two characters, one meaning *danger* and the other meaning *opportunity*. A crisis can therefore be looked upon as a dangerous opportunity. If you approach this idea properly, you can turn it to your advantage and leap ahead rapidly.

For example, many people lose their jobs through layoffs, mergers and acquisitions, and dismissal. The loss of a job is often devastating: some people take many months to recover and get back into the workforce. However, almost every great success in America was preceded by the unexpected loss of a job. Many self-made millionaires in America, in looking back, are extremely thankful that their previous job came to an end. They recognize that if they'd stayed there, they would never have achieved success. They were able to turn a crisis into an opportunity by looking for the good in a situation, and so can you.

The second part of the law of expectation says that whenever God sends you a gift, he wraps it up in a problem. This comes from the late inspirational author Norman Vincent Peale. He said that the bigger the gift that you're being sent, the bigger the problem it'll be wrapped up in. The low performer tends to focus on the problem, while the high performer tends to look past and through the problem for the gift or opportunity that it might contain. And the remarkable thing is, whatever you look for is what you'll find. If you look for the good or the gift or the opportunity, you will certainly find it.

The third part of this law says that you get what you expect, if you expect it long enough. Nature seems to put each of us to a test to see just how serious we really are about achieving the success we say we want, and the test is one of adversity and disappointment. The great majority of people collapse when things go wrong for them for any period of time. They demonstrate by their actions that they don't really believe the success they want is possible for them.

The small minority of high achievers, however, continue to expect the best and continue to expect that something good will come out of every difficulty, and in the long run they're seldom disappointed.

The Law of Opportunity

The fifth law of luck is the *law of opportunity*, which says that your greatest possibilities will come from the most common situations. Many people tend to look for their opportunities to come from some great distance or as the result of some remarkable stroke of good fortune. The fact is that most of your opportunities will lie very closely at hand. They're usually contained in your own background and experience, your own education and training, your own business or industry. Sometimes the opportunities you are seeking are within your current interests and hobbies. They'll almost invariably utilize your existing talents and abilities. Very often your opportunity comes by looking around you at the simplest things that are happening in your work.

The first part of the law of opportunity says that opportunities usually come dressed in work clothes, and opportunities seldom comes fully developed. Usually, it looks like a lot of hard work with no guarantee of success at the end. Sometimes a person will be offered a new job or a second income opportunity. He might turn it down because he says he's waiting for his big chance and he doesn't want to get his hands tied up. Often someone will offer a person a book or an audio program and the person will refuse to read it or listen to it without realizing that it could contain ideas that could set him or her on the road to riches.

The second part of the law of opportunity says that a wise person will create more opportunities than they find. Better yet, they will seize the opportunities by applying themselves to normal everyday events and will create opportunities that no one else sees. One of the richest men in America came up with the idea that there was oil in large pools in Texas and Oklahoma, several thousand feet below the shallower oil fields, which had already been tapped out. He bought up oil leases inexpensively and invested every dollar he could beg or borrow into his idea. He turned out to be right, and he struck huge quantities of oil by drilling deeper than anyone else ever had. He became one of the richest men in the world as a result. He made his opportunity when other people told him there was no more oil down there to be found.

The third part of the law of opportunity says that opportunities are like buses: there will always be another one along. This part of the law also says that you need not be stampeded into acting at a rate or speed with which you're not comfortable. Often it's better to let an opportunity go past and wait for the next one than to risk losing everything. Long-term money is patient money.

The Law of Ability

The sixth law of luck is the *law of ability*, which says that luck is preparedness meeting opportunity. The first part of this law says that the greater your ability in any area, the more luck you'll experience in that area.

Earl Nightingale once said that if you received an opportunity for which you weren't prepared and you tried to seize it anyway, you would only look foolish. By the law of attraction, whatever abilities you develop in yourself, you'll eventually get your opportunity to use those abilities to the fullest. Your job is to develop them in the first place. Your job is to soak yourself in every kind of information possible that might help you to achieve your goals when the time is right. Sooner or later you'll get your chance.

The second part of this law says that it's not enough to be in the right place at the right time; you must be the right *person* in the right place at the right time. When we look at men and women who have achieved major breakthroughs as a result of what appears to be luck, we find that those breakthroughs were preceded by weeks, months, and often many years of painstaking study that enabled them to be prepared when the door of opportunity opened.

The Law of Integrative Complexity

Seventh is the *law of integrative complexity*. This law says that the person with the widest variety of knowledge and skills in any area will tend to experience the most luck in that area. The individual who eventually wins in any situation will be the one who combines the greatest amount of information and knowledge into a coherent pattern for making decisions and acting. Sometimes knowing just one additional piece of information can be the turning point for you.

During the Civil War, General Robert E. Lee of the Army of Northern Virginia was said to have this kind of mind: the highest level of integrative complexity of any general on either side, Union or Confederate. As a result, he was able to defeat every general that was sent against him. He said the only thing that he really feared was that the Northern forces under Abraham Lincoln would finally find the general who could think better and faster than he could.

General Ulysses S. Grant was deemed to be the only general that the North ever put in command of an army against Lee who had a level of integrative complexity developed to the same height. Grant took over as commander of all Union forces in March 1864; a year later, the Confederacy was in ruins, the South was defeated, and the war was over.

You can develop ever higher levels of integrative complexity by continually adding to your store of knowledge. The first part of the law of integrative complexity says that the more you know, the more you grow. In fact, the more you learn, the more you're capable of learning. The more you work on your mind, the better and stronger it becomes.

The second part of this law says that the wider the net you throw, the bigger will be your catch. By the law of integrative complexity, continually gathering more and more knowledge increases the probabilities that you'll have the specific information or specific insight that will enable you to turn a situation to your advantage. Fear is and always has been the greatest enemy of mankind. It's only when you conquer fear that your mind opens up to all the possibilities that lie around you.

The Law of Assumption

The eighth law of luck is the *law of assumption*, which we've also talked about before. It says that incorrect assumptions lie at the root of every failure. Whenever you assume something to be true, you also assume that it has a certain degree of predictive validity: acting on that assumption will allow you to achieve certain objectives.

Incorrect assumptions lie at the root of every failure.

If you don't get what you expect, the first thing you must do is question your assumptions. This brings us to the first part of the law of assumption, which says the continuing assumption that you could be dead wrong is the key to getting it dead right. One of my favorite quotes is from Oliver Cromwell, Lord Protector of Great Britain in the seventeenth century. In an address to the British Parliament, he said, "I beseech you in the bowels of Christ, think it possible you may be mistaken." Cromwell was trying to get them to open their minds to a wider range of probabilities and explanations for the current situation.

Unfortunately, many people tend to slip into a mental comfort zone and become inflexible in their thinking. However, luck comes from allowing your mind to roam freely over all the possibilities of a situation. Consider that the correct thing to do might be the exact opposite of what you're doing right now. Luck often comes from being open to such possibilities, from challenging your assumptions.

The second part of this law says that questioning your assumptions will enable you to see possibilities that you might not have dreamed of. This is the hallmark of the adaptive, fluid, and flexible person. This is the divergent thinker. This is the person who speculates and who's willing to be childish, even ridiculous, in throwing out suggestions. One of the best questions that you can ask is *why*. Why are we doing it this way? Could there be a better way? Should we be doing it at all? If there were a better way, what might it be?

The Law of Timing

The ninth law is the *law of timing*, which is best summarized by these lines from Shakespeare's *Julius Caesar*: "There is a tide in the affairs of men / Which, taken at the flood, leads on to fortune."

Time is a fundamental aspect of luck or opportunity. In all of human affairs, there is both a too soon and a too late. Men and women who are described as lucky are invariably those who recognize when the time is right and move swiftly. In so doing, they sometimes save themselves months and years of hard work.

The first part of this law says that timing is everything. It also says that because of the law of attraction, you'll get what you are meant to get when you are ready and not before.

The second part of this law comes from Woody Allen, who said, "eighty percent of life is just showing up." Many successful people make a habit of being in as many places as possible to increase the probabilities of being in the right place at the right time.

The third part of the law of timing says that the more often you try, the more likely you are to triumph. You can put the law of averages to work in your favor by increasing the number of times that you attempt to achieve any goal.

The Law of Energy

The tenth law of luck is the *law of energy*, which says that the greater your energy and enthusiasm, the more likely you will be to recognize and respond to luck. The more energetic you are, the more likely you are to experience lucky occasions. Luck requires both having the opportunity and responding quickly to that opportunity, which requires energy.

The first part of this law says that alertness enables you to see roses where others only see thorns. When you are rested, refreshed, and alert, when you're physically fit in mind and body, you're much more likely to see possibilities that escape most other people.

The second part of the law of energy says that presence of mind and speed of action can turn ordinary events into stepping stones to success. Many men and women have changed the courses of their lives by seizing an opportunity quickly when it arose. Sometimes it was with careful thought, and sometimes it was simply spontaneous, but these individuals had high energy and acted or spoke quickly when the chance occurred.

Very often, your great peace of luck can come after a string of setbacks and disappointments. The law of probability says that you're entitled to a lucky break if you've had a series of unlucky occurrences. Be ready for the tide to turn so that you can move with it quickly when it does.

The third part of the law of energy says that when the night becomes darkest, the stars come out. When things seem to be the very worst, if you bide your time and await your chance, your opportunity will sometimes occur. Be ready to seize it and respond quickly. During the darkest days of World War II, members of Winston Churchill's cabinet were urging him to make peace with Hitler. He refused to do so and insisted that something would happen to bring America into the war if they just held on long enough. Even though Franklin D. Roosevelt had been reelected in 1940 by promising not to involve the United States in another war in Europe, Churchill believed that something would happen that would change everything if he held on long enough.

On December 7, 1941, the Japanese on the other side of the world launched a surprise attack on Pearl Harbor. When Adolf Hitler heard about the surprise attack, he had to ask one of his generals where Pearl Harbor was. He had no idea of the geography of the Pacific; nevertheless, Hitler declared war on the United States.

Roosevelt went before Congress and asked for a declaration of war on Japan, and, because of Germany's declaration, for a declaration of war on Germany as well. From that moment on, America would be supporting England. Winston Churchill had turned out to be right once again; his luck had turned.

The Law of Relationships

Eleventh is the *law of relationships* as it applies to luck. It says that the number of people you know and who know you will determine your luck as much as any other factor.

The first part of this law says that most luck arises from your contacts with other people and from their decision and desire to help you.

Most luck arises from contacts with other people.

The second part of this law says that chance remarks can change the direction of your life. Luck is often contained in comments from friendly strangers you meet in passing. Sometimes a person will make an observation or pass along a fact that is the critical part of the puzzle you're trying to solve.

Mark Twain once wrote that his whole life was changed when a piece of paper containing a short essay blew against his leg when he was walking down the streets of Hannibal, Missouri, as a young man. He picked up the paper, which someone had dropped, and read it, and it changed him forever. Sometimes someone can suggest that you read a book or take a course or meet a particular person; pay particular attention to these inputs. Remember, what you want, wants you. Your luck will often appear in the guise of a stranger. Be alert to the fact that luck is often very playful and comes to you in a joking manner from a direction that you least expect. Keep an open mind and be willing to pursue these chance circumstances.

The third part of this law as it applies to luck is that when the student is ready, the master will appear. This is another example of the laws of attraction, expectation, cause and effect and many other laws. When you develop a divine discontent and you're sincerely committed to changing and improving your life, someone or something will appear, possibly in the form of a book, an audio, a course, or a teacher, and will give you the critical piece of information that you need at that time.

The Law of Empathy

The twelfth law of luck is the *law of empathy*. It says that if you can see the situation through the eyes of the other person, your perspective can reveal unseen possibilities. This is especially true in business, sales, and all personal relationships. Stephen R. Covey said, seek first to understand, then to be understood. Make every effort to view the situation from the perspective of the other person, and you'll often see things you would have missed otherwise.

The first part of the law of empathy is the old Indian saying: walk a mile in the other person's moccasins. When you develop a deep sense of empathy for the problems, difficulties, and needs of other people, you'll often see how you can satisfy them in a way that no one has ever thought of before.

The second part of this law, which is a key to success in business, says simply that if you can see John Jones through John Jones' eyes, you can sell John Jones what John Jones buys. Ask yourself, what is his perspective? What does this person see? What does this person want and what is he willing to pay for?

When you put all these different laws together, you begin to realize that luck is largely predictable and you can dramatically increase the incidents of it that you enjoy in your life. You can bring the powers and forces of nature together to work for you to help you achieve your goals. Luck and good fortune will increase in every area of your life if you'll simply do the things that we've discussed and developed the qualities practiced by other lucky and successful people. Good luck!

The Laws of Luck

The law of probability. There is a mathematical probability of the occurrence of any event which can be deduced with considerable accuracy from observation, measurement, and experience.

The law of clarity. The clearer you are about what you want and what you're willing to do to get it, the greater the probability that you'll experience luck.

The law of attraction. You inevitably attract into your life the people, ideas, circumstances, and resources that harmonize with your dominant thoughts.

The law of expectations. You can increase the amount of luck in your life by continually expecting lucky things to happen.

The law of opportunity. Your greatest possibilities will come from the most common situations.

The law of ability. Luck is preparedness meeting opportunity.

The law of integrative complexity. The person with the widest variety of knowledge and skills in any area will tend to experience the most luck in that area.

The law of assumption. Incorrect assumptions lie at the root of every failure.

The law of timing. The right timing is the key to opportunity.

The law of energy. The greater your energy and enthusiasm, the more likely you will be to recognize and respond to luck.

The law of relationships. The number of people you know and who know you will determine your luck as much as any other factor.

The law of empathy. If you can see the situation through the eyes of the other person, your perspective can reveal unseen possibilities.

twelve

The Laws of Self-Fulfillment

Perhaps your greatest responsibility to yourself, and your most important job in life, is to become everything you're capable of becoming and realize your full potential as a human being. It's to achieve your personal best and to become the best person that you can be in every area of your life. True happiness and lasting satisfaction only come when you feel that you're living your life to the fullest, you're working on the outer edge of your capabilities, and you're stretching yourself to become more than you've ever been in the past.

Throughout this book, I've introduced you to a series of laws and principles that are timeless and applicable to virtually every area of your life. Some of them have been repeated in different ways and with different applications. These laws largely explain what happens to you or what fails to happen. Some are general and affect virtually every area of your life, like the law of cause and effect. Some are more particular and are often specific to a single activity or area of endeavor, like money or wealth creation.

One of the most important of the laws that I've talked about is the law of belief. Your beliefs have such an inordinate impact on your thinking that you don't so much believe what you see, but you see what you believe. Your beliefs form the master program of your subconscious computer, and you can seldom exceed your deeply held convictions concerning your own capabilities. You can rarely do more than you think you can or be more than you believe you can.

**Your beliefs form the master program
of your subconscious computer.**

The wonderful thing is that because of the law of reversibility, by taking actions consistent with the beliefs about yourself that you want to have, the actions themselves have a backflow effect that causes you to believe that way. This itself is a core principle of self-fulfillment.

The law of expectation says that whatever you expect with confidence becomes your own self-fulfilling prophecy. You live out your true expectations in virtually everything that you say and do. The law of correspondence says that your outer world tends to mirror your inner world. What you see on the outside of your life is largely a reflection of what's going on in the inside.

Perhaps the most powerful law of all is what we can call the law of the universe: the law of superconscious activity, which says that any thought, plan, goal, or idea that you can hold continually in your conscious mind must be brought into reality by your super-conscious mind. If you absolutely believe that something is possible for you and you hold to that belief tenaciously, you activate the entire power of the universe behind your chosen dreams and goals. You can then go on to accomplish more in a short time than many people accomplish in a lifetime.

In this book, I'll explain thirteen additional laws of self-fulfillment and how they work in your life. Applying these laws or any combination of them will help you to have, do, and be more than you ever could without them.

The Law of Growth

The first law of fulfillment is the *law of growth*. This law states that if you're not growing, you are stagnating. Change is the only constant factor in life. You can avoid taxes by not working, and you can avoid death for a long time by taking excellent care of your physical health. Nevertheless, we're all caught up in the turbulence of continuous change, and the successful men and women of today and tomorrow are change masters. It's only when you learn to welcome change, embrace change, and continually grow from change that you free yourself from the danger of being bowled over by changes over which you have little control.

All progress and improvement require change. I've emphasized the importance of clear goals throughout this book in part because goals enable you to control the direction of change. Goals assure that change will be predominantly positive and constructive. If change is unavoidable and inevitable, you want to be sure that whatever changes are taking place are helping you in some way, which requires goals.

The Law of Practice

The second law of self-fulfillment is the *law of practice*, which says whatever you practice over and over again and often enough becomes a new habit. With this law, you can control your destiny and the kind of person you become. Your entire evolution and growth as a human being depend upon the fact that your character is not fixed in place. It's fluid and capable of growth and development. You can become what you want to become. With practice, you can develop the habit of arising early in the morning and planning your day thoroughly before you begin. You can develop the habit of self-discipline. You can develop the habit of aggressiveness, purposefulness, and whatever else you desire.

The first part of the law of practice is a peak performance technique called *mental rehearsal.* This technique is used by the top athletes, top businesspeople, and virtually all high-achieving men and women in our society. The principle of mental rehearsal says that you can develop any habit pattern of action or behavior you desire by practicing it repeatedly in your mind prior to the situation that requires it. For example, if you have an upcoming meeting with your boss or banker, you can go through the entire meeting mentally and practice being calm, confident, and relaxed throughout.

The second part of this law says that the more relaxed you are when you visualize a new behavior, the more rapidly it's accepted by your subconscious mind and the more rapidly you will begin to act consistently with your mental picture. This law of practice and the need to mentally rehearse in a deeply relaxed state is called *autogenic conditioning* or *autosuggestion.* It's perhaps the most powerful peak performance technique available to you without training. All you have to do to use it is to create a mental movie of exactly how you want a particular situation to work out. Play that movie over and over again in your mind prior to the situation, and you'll be amazed at how often everything happens exactly the way you imagined.

The third part of the law of practice says that you must launch new habits and behaviors strongly. Never allow an exception before the new habit is fully entrenched. Once you decide to utilize the law of practice and develop a new behavior or attitude to override or replace an old behavior or attitude, you must discipline yourself to stay with it until the new habit is firmly in place. For example, if you decide to get up at 6:00 a.m. every morning, you must force yourself to do it over and over again until you wake up automatically at 6:00 a.m. and can't get back to sleep. This isn't easy in any area, but it can make a tremendous difference to your level of self-fulfillment.

The Law of Accumulation

The third law of self-fulfillment is the *law of accumulation*, which says that every great life is an accumulation of hundreds and thousands of efforts and sacrifices that no one else sees or appreciates. I've discussed this law before, and it's absolutely essential if you want to be all you can be. We all start off with limited knowledge and resources; only through the long, hard process of accumulation, like a snowball gathering snowflakes as it rolls down a hill, do we build ourselves up to the point where we're capable of fulfilling our aspirations.

Every great life is an accumulation of hundreds and thousands of efforts and sacrifices.

This law also says that no worthwhile effort or sacrifice is ever lost. You may have to work for many weeks, months, or even years before you begin to see the results of this process, but every good thing you do, every extra effort you make, is accumulating and becoming part of your character and your future.

I have already discussed the importance of time perspective: taking the long view with regard to your life and making short-term sacrifices for long-term gains. Other people will often try to discourage and dissuade you and get you to put off these efforts in favor of having fun in the present, but you must ignore them and persevere regardless. The law of accumulation is another iron law of success and personal fulfillment. Anyone who violates it ends up paying the price by living a life far below their capabilities.

The Law of Incremental Improvement

The fourth law of self-fulfillment is the *law of incremental improvement*. This is a sublaw of the law of accumulation. It says that mastery and excellence in any field are the results of countless efforts of self-development over an extended period of time. You need to invest countless hours of working on yourself and on your profession or occupation to reach the point where you begin to enjoy the big rewards. No matter where you start, your future potential is unlimited through this law of incremental improvement. It's the key to self-fulfillment, because happiness in life is a journey, not a destination.

As I said before, happiness is the progressive, step-by-step realization of a worthy ideal. A feeling of personal growth towards something that's important to the individual is the root cause of motivation, enthusiasm, and excitement about life.

The first part of the law of accumulation comes from a quote variously attributed to the great pianist Ignacy Jan Paderewski, who also became the prime minister of Poland, and to the master violinist Jascha Heifetz. In any case, when this master musician was asked why he continued to practice, he replied with these classic words: "If I don't practice for even one day, I know the difference. If I don't practice for two days, the critics know the difference, and if I don't practice for three days, the public knows the difference."

It's always obvious to anyone who's looking whether or not you're engaged in this ongoing process of incremental improvement. The late comedian and actor George Burns did his routine for decades, going back to the days of vaudeville back in the twenties. He was regularly booked to perform before large audiences, yet prior to every single performance, he spent one solid hour of review and rehearsal alone in his dressing room, even though he had done the same material hundreds if not thousands of times. He was always working on it to keep it fresh and improve it in some way.

The second part of the law of incremental improvement is what I call Longfellow's law. This comes from the immortal words of the poet Henry Wadsworth Longfellow, who said, "Those heights by great men reached and kept were not achieved by sudden flight, / But they while their companions slept, were toiling upward in the night."

The Law of Self-Development

Fifth is the *law of self-development*: you can become whatever you want in life if you'll just learn what you need to know in order to achieve it. You don't have to be envious of the accomplishments of anyone else: whatever anyone else has done that you sincerely wish to do yourself, you can learn to do if you apply yourself long enough and hard enough. By the law of self-development, you can raise yourself by your own bootstraps to any height that you desire.

Here's an exercise for you: Project yourself forward in time and see yourself living your ideal lifestyle, surrounded by the kind of people, work, and material things that you most desire. From this mental vantage point, look back to the present and imagine the steps you might take and the things you might have to learn in order to get to where you want to be. This exercise is amazingly effective in clarifying the things that you're going to have to do and become. Starting today, to get to wherever you want to go in the future, just give it a try.

The Law of Talents

The sixth law of self-fulfillment is the *law of talents*. It says that your greatest opportunities lie in the development and exploitation of your inborn talents and abilities. You don't need to become a different person or develop different capabilities. You merely need to dig deep down into the gold mine of your own potentials, and you'll find riches enough to build any kind of life you might want.

The first part of the law of talents is what I call *Gardner's observation*, after the work of Howard Gardner on human potential. It says simply, you are a genius. Because of the unique structure of your brain, you have the capacity to perform at exceptional levels in an area that interests you so much that you become totally absorbed by your activities in that area.

Gardner has demonstrated that there are at least seven major forms of intelligence, and that each person is blessed with a combination of these different forms of intelligence, the proper use of which can make you unstoppable.

The second part of the law of talents is the parable of Jesus where he talks about talents: "Thou good and faithful servant, thou hast been faithful over a few things, I will make thee ruler over many things" (Matthew 25:21). This is another way of saying that as you stretch your existing talents and abilities, you'll be given ample opportunities to use even more of them.

The third part of the law of talents is what I call Rohn's recommendation, from business philosopher Jim Rohn, who said, "If you work on your gifts, they will make way for you." This is a wonderful truth tied into the law of talents. If you go to work on the innate abilities that you've identified already, your capabilities will begin to expand and enable you to embrace all kinds of other opportunities.

The fourth part of the law of talents is what I call *Rothschild's revision*, after the elder Baron de Rothschild, who became one of the world's wealthiest men by practicing certain principles in his own business life. His original rule was, "Make no useless acquaintances." My revision says, learn no useless subjects or skills. All you really have to trade is your time. You trade time for the kind of life you'll enjoy in the future. Refuse to spend hours or weeks learning a subject simply because it's fun and enjoyable. Instead, use those same hours to develop your talents and abilities, to develop yourself personally and professionally, and to activate the laws of accumulation and incremental improvement, so that you become an outstanding human being.

The Law of Excellence

The seventh law of self-fulfillment is the *law of excellence*: the quality of your life will be determined by the depth of your commitment to excellence more than by any other factor. The foundation of a great life is to achieve excellence at doing something that's important to you.

The quality of your life will be determined by the depth of your commitment to excellence.

It's only when you're really good at what you're doing that you feel like a winner, that you enjoy high self-esteem and a tremendous feeling of self-respect and self-fulfillment. Conversely, you can't feel very good about yourself simply by doing a job in an average or mediocre way.

Your aim should be to be outstanding at the important things you do. If you're in sales, your goal should be to be among the top 20 percent of salespeople in your field. If you're already there, you should aim to be in the top 10 percent (as defined by income).

The first part of the law of excellence comes from inspirational philosopher Émile Coué. It's a paraphrase of his famous advice, which was to say, "Every day in every way, I'm getting better and better." Similarly, you should be saying to yourself, "Every day in every way, I'm getting better and better in my chosen field." If you're not getting better and better, then reorganize your life so that you read books, attend courses, and listen to audios until you are.

The second part of the law of excellence comes from John Palmer of the National Speakers Bureau, who was once asked what it took to get ahead in a competitive field. He replied with these wonderful words: "Get good, get better, be the best. Never be satisfied with anything less than being at the top." As football coach Red Sanders said, "Winning is not everything. It's the only thing."

The third part of this law of excellence comes from the great football coach Bear Bryant, who said, "It's not the will to win that matters—everyone has that. It's the will to prepare." In coaching winning football teams, he noticed that virtually everybody wanted to win, but that only a few players wanted it badly enough to put in the exhaustive preparation necessary. Everybody wants to be the best, but very few people are willing to make the efforts necessary to be the best. If you decide to be the best and you combine that with the necessary work, nothing can stop you.

The Law of Opportunity

The eighth law of self-fulfillment is the *law of opportunity*. This version comes from Napoleon Hill, who discovered after a lifetime of research on success that within every setback or obstacle there lies the seed of an equal or greater benefit or opportunity. He found that the most successful men and women lived by this law and took every setback as a spur to greater effort.

The first part of the law of opportunity refers to your level of confidence. It says that the more confidence you have in your ultimate ability to succeed, the more boldly you will act on opportunities when they arise. When you tune your mind to success and develop a prosperity consciousness, when you begin to apply the law of abundance to the world around you, you'll see more opportunities than you can possibly take advantage of. Being confident that everything that you're doing is propelling you towards your goals will cause you to make more progress than other people around you.

The second part of the law of opportunity refers back to the law of reversibility: just as your feelings dictate your thoughts and actions, your actions have a reverse effect and create your thoughts and feelings. If you want to be enthusiastic, pretend that you're already enthusiastic, and the pretense will soon generate enthusiasm. You'll be amazed at how many more opportunities you become aware of just by acting as though you expect to discover them.

The Law of Courage

Ninth is what I earlier called the *law of courage*. In this context, it says that if you confront the thing you fear, the death of fear is certain. The greatest single obstacle to self-fulfillment is and always has been fear, combined with ignorance. It's fear of failure, fear of criticism, fear of poverty, fear of losing, fear of disapproval, and every other kind of fear that acts as a brake on becoming the kind of person you want to become.

Men and women with leadership qualities always turn toward the things they fear and in so doing, face them down. They never avoid fearful situations or people. They look upon fear as an enemy to be challenged, confronted, and dealt with rather than evaded or ignored.

The first part of the law of courage comes from the Latin adage *carpe diem*, which means, *seize the day*. The second part says, act as if it were impossible to fail, and it shall be. You can develop the courage that makes you unstoppable by simply disciplining yourself to act courageously even when deep down inside you don't feel it. There seems to be a direct relationship between your willingness to face the disapproval of strangers and your ability to get ahead.

If you're single and you see an attractive member of the opposite sex you'd like to meet, just walk up and introduce yourself. If you're in sales, you can overcome the fear that holds many salespeople back by simply forcing yourself to go out and call on new prospects until the fear finally disappears. In every case, you'll feel far better about yourself when you confront your fears squarely and move ahead confidently in the direction of your dreams.

The Law of Applied Effort

The tenth law of self-fulfillment is *the law of applied effort*. It says that all great achievement is preceded and accompanied by hard work. Thomas Stanley's research into the lifestyles of thousands of affluent Americans found that virtually every one of them ascribe their success to the ability to work harder than anyone else.

The first part of the law of applied effort is what I call *Getty's principle*. John Paul Getty became the richest man in the world of his time. He was a millionaire by the age of twenty-three and a billionaire two decades later. When he was asked the secret of his success, he replied with just two words: "Try harder." The journalist asked him what he would do if that didn't work, and he replied simply that he would try harder still. Almost all things are amenable to hard work.

If you're not getting the results that you want, simply try harder. It's been said that the best sales come at the end of the longest day, at the end of the longest street, to the very last person you call on. When you work well beyond what anyone could expect, you feel the best about yourself and you really start to get results.

The second part of this law of applied effort is simply this: work all the time you work; don't view your work as a social occasion or a place to fool around. Be serious. While you're working, don't drop off your dry cleaning, pick up your groceries, or wash your car. Don't talk on the telephone with your friends and family, and don't socialize around the water cooler. Get a reputation instead for being the kind of person who works all the time they work. Try it and see. You'll be amazed at the results.

The Law of Giving

The eleventh law of self-fulfillment is *the law of giving*. With the Bible, this law states that it is more blessed to give than to receive. It's more profitable as well. Life today belongs to the *go-giver* rather than the go-getter. All around you, you'll see both givers and takers, and you'll find that the givers are the most popular and successful in everything they do and wherever they go.

The law of giving is tied into the law of service, which says that you can only achieve real meaning and purpose to the degree to which you feel that you're serving other people in some way.

You can only achieve real meaning and purpose to the degree to which you feel that you're serving other people.

The first part of this law says that the only gift worth giving is that which includes the giver. It's the part of yourself that you attach to any gift that makes it valuable. A favorite stone given by a child is a far more important gift than something given out of obligation or with indifference.

The second part of this law is that the more of yourself that you give without expectation of return, the greater will be your return, often from the most unexpected sources. Almost everyone has discovered that when they give of themselves to others, good things come back to them from the most unexpected directions.

It's a basic rule that the person you help is never the person that pays you back. It's often someone else who helps you at a different time and place and in a different way. But it was the initial willingness to give of yourself that created this force field of energy that led to someone else helping you when you were in need.

The third part of this law is the principle of reciprocity, which says that whenever you give or do something nice for another person, you trigger within that person the desire to reciprocate. None of us wants to feel under obligation to another, so when someone does something nice for us, we feel a need to do something nice back to even the score. The smart person is always looking for ways to do things for others, knowing that the gift will inevitably come back and sometimes in far greater measure than what was put out.

The fourth part of giving has to do with timing. A single rose, given at the right time, can be worth a dozen roses given too late. This is one of my favorite quotes: "I shall pass this way but once; any good that I can do or any kindness I can show to any human being, let me do it now. Let me not defer nor neglect it, for I shall not pass this way again."

The Law of Affirmation

The twelfth law here is the *law of affirmation*: whatever you repeat to yourself often enough will eventually be accepted by your subconscious mind as a fact and will become a part of your beliefs. By affirming to yourself over and over any dream, desire, or goal that you wish, you eventually come to believe it and accept it as an inevitable truth for you. At that point, it takes on a force of its own and begins moving you irresistibly towards it, and it toward you.

The law of affirmation is based on the three P's. The first P stands for *positive*: "I can do it, I can do it, I can do it." The second P stands for *personal*. You always use the word *I* rather than *you* or *we* or *they*. You say, "I like myself, I like myself, I like myself." The third P stands for *present*. Always phrase your affirmations in the present tense. You can say, "I feel terrific" rather than "I will feel terrific tomorrow." Your subconscious mind can only be accessed by words that are programmed in personal, present, and positive terms.

The first part of the law of affirmation is that the most powerful words of all are the ones you say to yourself and believe. The more often you repeat them to yourself and the more emotionally you say them, the more you believe them to be true. The more you believe them, the more of an impact they'll have on your thinking and behavior.

The second part of the law of affirmation is that the most powerful affirmation is visualization. Whenever you visualize and combine that mental picture with the emotion of desire, it's passed rapidly as a command from your conscious mind to your subconscious mind, and it begins to activate the laws of attraction, expectation, correspondence, and many other laws. What you see on the inside, you begin to experience on the outside. This is perhaps the most amazing power that a human being can have.

The third part of this law simply says that with affirmations, both verbal and visual, your potential is unlimited.

The Law of Optimism

Finally, the thirteenth law of self-fulfillment is the *law of optimism*, which says that a positive mental attitude is closely associated with success in virtually every area of life. The more positive and optimistic you are, the more constructive your thoughts and behaviors, the more likely you are to achieve greatness in everything you attempt.

The first part of the law of optimism says that you think, feel, and act the way you do because of the way you interpret experiences and events to yourself. The way you talk to yourself about the way you think things are happening has an inordinate impact on how positive you feel. If you slip and begin talking to yourself in a negative way, it will cast a pall of gloom over your whole personality, so watch your words and your inner dialogue. Be careful about your conversation and the way you talk about how you feel about events around you.

The second part of the law of optimism says that every thought, feeling, word, or action you engage in is a choice made by yourself for which you are totally responsible. Since no one can think and decide for you but yourself, you are completely responsible for the results of your thinking. Since no one controls your inner dialogue but yourself, the starting point of optimism and happiness is to think what you want to think and make sure that your thoughts are continually on the person you want to be and the things you want to accomplish.

Let me leave you with this important idea. There are exceptions to many of these laws. Sometimes they seem not to work at all in the short term. It's easy for a person to challenge a law that might require him to change his thinking or actions by pointing out the exceptions to the law and using them to attempt to invalidate the law. This, unfortunately, is a method of crooked thinking, and it's harmful in that it often leads a person away from the very things they need to know and practice to achieve the goals they've set for themselves.

The keys to mental well-being and happiness are a sense of control and a sense of coherence, which go hand in hand. You experience a sense of control to the degree to which you accept complete responsibility as the cause of the effects in your life.

In explaining the role your thinking plays in determining your life, these laws put you into the driver's seat. Because you control your thinking, and your thinking controls your life, you are the master of your own destiny. The best way to organize your life is to obey these laws and confidently assume that they are continually at work.

You now have the laws of the universe and the secrets of the ages. There is nothing that you cannot do and be if you make up your mind and then just do it.

The Laws of Self-Fulfillment

The law of growth. If you're not growing, you are stagnating.

The law of practice. Whatever you practice over and over again and often enough becomes a new habit.

The law of accumulation. Every great life is an accumulation of hundreds and thousands of efforts and sacrifices that no one else sees or appreciates.

The law of incremental improvement. Mastery and excellence in any field are the results of countless efforts of self-development over an extended period of time.

The law of self-development. You can become whatever you want in life if you'll just learn what you need to know in order to achieve it.

The law of talents. Your greatest opportunities lie in the development and exploitation of your inborn talents and abilities.

The law of excellence. The quality of your life will be determined by the depth of your commitment to excellence more than by any other factor.

The law of opportunity. Within every setback or obstacle there lies the seed of an equal or greater benefit or opportunity.

The law of courage. If you confront the thing you fear, the death of fear is certain.

The law of applied effort. All great achievement is preceded and accompanied by hard work.

The law of giving. It is more blessed to give than to receive. It's more profitable as well.

The law of affirmation. Whatever you repeat to yourself often enough will eventually be accepted by your subconscious mind as a fact and will become a part of your beliefs.

The law of optimism. A positive mental attitude is closely associated with success in virtually every area of life.

Printed in the USA
CPSIA information can be obtained
at www.ICGtesting.com
JSHW010852081224
74960JS00005B/6